Dawson's Creek

™

THE OFFICIAL COMPANION
Darren Crosdale

Based on the hit television series
created by Kevin Williamson

Andrews McMeel
Publishing
Kansas City

This edition was originally published in Great Britain in 1999

Dawson's Creek: The Official Companion copyright © 1999 by Columbia TriStar
Television, Inc. Episodes 201–206 © 1999 Global Entertainment Productions
GmbH & Co. Medien KG. All rights reserved. Printed in the United States of
America. No part of this book may be used or reproduced in any manner
whatsoever without written permission except in the case of reprints in the
context of reviews. For information, write Andrews McMeel Publishing, 4520
Main Street, Kansas City, Missouri 64111.

www. andrewsmcmeel.com

99 00 01 02 03 QUF 10 9 8 7 6 5 4 3 2 1

ISBN: 0-7407-0725-6

Library of Congress Catalog Card Number: 99-67644

ATTENTION: SCHOOLS AND BUSINESSES
Andrews McMeel books are available at quantity discounts with bulk purchase
for educational, business, or sales promotional use. For information, please write
to: Special Sales Department, Andrews McMeel Publishing, 4520 Main Street,
Kansas City, Missouri 64111.

First published in UK in 1999 by
Ebury Press
Random House, 20 Vauxhall Bridge Road, London SW1V 2SA

Random House Australia Pty Limited
20 Alfred Street, Milsons Point, Sydney, New South Wales 2061, Australia

Random House New Zealand Limited
18 Poland Road, Glenfield, Auckland 10, New Zealand

Random House South Africa (Pty) Limited
Endulini, 5A Jubilee Road, Parktown 2193, South Africa

Random House UK Limited Reg. No. 954009

Design by Dan Newman

Front cover photo by Guy D'Alema
Inside photos by Guy D'Alema, Marc Kayne, Fred Norris, and Frank Ockenfels

THE OFFICIAL COMPANION

Darren Crosdale

Based on the hit television series created by Kevin Williamson

Andrews McMeel
Publishing

Kansas City

www.andrewsmcmeel.com

99 00 01 02 03 QUF 10 9 8 7 6 5 4 3 2 1

ISBN: 0-7407-0725-6

Library of Congress Catalog Card Number: 99-67644

First published in UK in 1999 by
Ebury Press
Random House, 20 Vauxhall Bridge Road, London SW1V 2SA

Random House Australia Pty Limited
20 Alfred Street, Milsons Point, Sydney, New South Wales 2061, Australia

Random House New Zealand Limited
18 Poland Road, Glenfield, Auckland 10, New Zealand

Random House South Africa (Pty) Limited
Endulini, 5A Jubilee Road, Parktown 2193, South Africa

Random House UK Limited Reg. No. 954009

Design by Dan Newman

Front cover photo by Guy D'Alema
Inside photos by Guy D'Alema, Marc Kayne, Fred Norris, and Frank Ockenfels

Contents

Introduction:
The Cascade Begins

At last – there's an indispensable Official Guide to *Dawson's Creek* – the show of this and that millennium. *Dawson's Creek* captures people's attention. Big time. The ingredients are all there for a successful show: great dialogue, good-looking cast, high production values. With the speed of word-of-mouth, it quickly became the number one show among teen girls on American TV. Sure, there had been shows about teens stumbling their way through young adulthood before. We had the sensitive ones like *My So-Called Life*, the not-so-realistic shows such as *Beverly Hills, 90210* and the super-realistic ones like MTV's *The Real World*. But with Dawson, Joey, Pacey, and Jen, there is something more pertinent. It's so engaging it makes you rush home, sit on the edge of your seat and if you're denied your own television, squabble over the remote control.

Jen Lindley, gentle and alluring, turns up and rocks a boat, which before her arrival only had room for three others in it. With his perma-grin, Pacey Witter gives the illusion that he always has something to laugh about. Beautifully brooding, Joey Potter always plays her cards very close to her heart. And of course, there's Dawson Leery, gorgeous and garrulous with a great line in psychoanalysis.

The show's appeal, though, lies in more than just the skin-crawling uncomfortable moments where characters and viewers alike wish the earth would open up and swallow them. Everyone is super smart and seems to have a one-liner for every occasion but – like all of us – life sporadically erupts into situations that leave them dumbstruck. Even with their quips and immaculate hair, they take time to recover. We're just like the folks on television. We've grown up with psychobabble and could psychologically deconstruct someone in a minute, but that does not mean we're immune to life's adventures. Just like the characters on the screen, we have perhaps tripped and scraped a knee on those first stumbling steps into the areas of love and romance.

The smooth-flowing creek pauses at the lives of parents, teachers, and grandparents. It reminds us that life's little lessons continue to be taught even after those last teen years have escaped us and one's skin is not as taut.

Dawson's Creek has such a universal appeal, it manages to break free of its expected demographic. It may center on the lives of teens by the seaside but its appeal is incalculably wider. Parents who have watched the show are able to reminisce on their own teen angst, the first kiss and the attendant sweaty palms. Who knows, the show may even aid adults in their efforts to relate to the twisting and turning roller-coaster journey their offspring are currently traveling.

Television viewers are often described as cynical. Trends are so fast-changing we're seen as couch potatoes who stare at flickering television screens with small sneers of incredulity and detachment splashed across our faces. But with *Dawson's Creek*, such preconceptions are brushed aside. Watching *Dawson's Creek* we smile, grin, grimace, frown, and some of us even shed a tear or three. We cannot help but care. We want Dawson to succeed in his film-making dreams. We desire – as much as Joey – the confidence she strives for. Pacey's need for familial support moves us as much as Jen's search for self.

Dawson's Creek viewers talk about the whos and the whats of the show at school, at college, and at work. Conversations about the psychological and emotional compatibility of Dawson and Joey reach lava-like temperatures. The will-they? won't-they? couple of the millennium have equal amounts of supporters and detractors. We telephone the uninitiated to remind them to watch the show. Earnest fans create web sites in honor of the show and surfers view these sites habitually.

All of these things help to make *Dawson's Creek* a show like no other, but there are intangible elements also. The sympathetic background of some of the most beautiful scenery ever filmed; a modern musical accompaniment that fits the emotions flitting across the screen like a tailored glove; the ebb and flow of realistic story lines.

It might be presumptuous to claim teens accept the show's voice – but viewing figures support this assertion. *The Wonder Years*, *Party of Five*, *My So-Called Life* and *Beverly Hills, 90210* – all of these shows spoke with a teen voice we could relate to. But none were as articulate, as energetic, as hilarious, as poignant, or as unmissable as *Dawson's Creek*.

This book reveals how *Dawson's Creek* captivates its viewers so completely. It delights in its multifaceted appeal and delves into the depths of the weekly emotional whirlpool. With exclusive interviews and unparalleled detail, it delineates the episodes, the angst, the awe, the hunky hubris, the tears, the joy, the babes, and the heart-stopping kisses that have swayed millions.

Dawson's Creek pays tribute to those moments of epiphany when life confusingly reveals itself to be neither as complicated nor as simplistic as misconstrued. Long may the Creek flow on.

Dawson's Creek Guide

SEASON 1

Dawson's Creek Pilot . . . . Episode #100
Teleplay written by Kevin Williamson
Directed by Steve Miner

If ever the debut episode of a new show laid it on the line – this one did. Anyone expecting a run-of-the-mill American teen drama was in for a big and pleasant surprise.

Dawson Leery (James Van Der Beek) and his best friend Joey Potter (Katie Holmes) are lying on his bed watching *E.T.* It's obvious Friday night is movie night, a regular occurrence. Joey once slept over regularly but is now hesitant. "Things change. I have breasts and you have genitalia!" Dawson's always had genitalia but Joey reckons "there's more of it now." Hormones rage and though always friends, Joey asserts they're no longer naïve kids. She wants to ensure they remain pals in spite of the "male/female thing." Dawson's incredulous – after all, he can tell her *everything*.

The next day, shooting a scary movie for a film festival, Dawson's directing Joey and Pacey Witter, his other best friend (Joshua Jackson). Filming pauses when the threesome spies a young girl climbing out of a taxi. Jennifer Lindley (Michelle Williams) has everything but a halo. The sun transforms her blonde hair into a beacon, her light summer dress billows around her shapely body. Dawson's transfixed. Joey is not. But what is the problem, after all, Joey and Dawson are just best friends, right? Jen has left New York to live with her Grams, Mrs. Ryan (Mary Beth Peil), and help look after her sick grandfather. She'll be attending Capeside High School.

At Screenplay Video, the store where he and Dawson work, Pacey flirts with a foxy older woman as she rents *The Graduate*. At school, the foxy lady is actually Miss Jacobs, Pacey's new English teacher. He's never paid so much attention in class. A trip to the movies is wrecked by Joey's attitude. She asks the intruder Jen if she's a virgin. Fortunately, Jen can handle herself and unashamedly confesses she is a virgin. Rebuffed by Miss Jacobs at the

Dawson to Jen:
"Whenever I have a problem, all I have to do is look to the right Spielberg movie and the answer is revealed."

Opposite: Dawson explains E.T.'s attraction to a rapt Joey

movies, Pacey bumps into her walking home. Self-assured, he declares: "I'm the best sex you'll never have!" Miss Jacobs grabs and kisses Pacey before running off ashamed.

Episode Music

"Run Like Mad" – Jann Arden (Season 1 theme song)
"As I Lay Me Down" – Sophie B. Hawkins
"Tubthumping" – Chumbawumba
"Mercy Me" – Say-So
"Good Mother" – Jann Arden
"Hey Pretty Girl" – Bodeans
"I'll Stand By You" – Pretenders

Later, Dawson insists he's able to tell Joey anything but she deftly proves him wrong by asking how often he "walks his dog." Dawson has no dog – not the four-legged kind anyway. Joey departs, sad her point has been proven. Dawson shouts: "Usually in the morning!" as she is on her way home. She smiles thinking their friendship may survive intact after all. Turning around, she spots Dawson's mom smooching her square-jawed co-anchor, Bob. Dawson has seen none of this and remains completely unaware of the traumas that await him.

Right: In the pilot episode, Jen Lindley captivates Dawson's imagination

Opposite: Miss Tamara Jacobs

Dance .... Episode #101

Teleplay written by Kevin Williamson
Directed by Steve Miner

Most 15-year-olds would not have the need for prosthetic heads, but then again, Dawson is unlike most 15-year-olds.

Showing Joey a prosthetic head in her likeness he created for the movie, Dawson praises her lush lips. She's flattered, considering how lifelike the head is. After Dawson confesses he has yet to kiss Jen, Joey warns him. "Don't wait an eternity. She is from New York where things tend to move faster."

Dawson learns his film class is working on a film written by, directed by, and starring the school hunk, Cliff Elliott. After Dawson declines Jen's invitation to the school dance, he sees her flirting with the long-fingered varsity quarterback Cliff whose invitation she does accept. Dawson's wounded and Joey admonishes: "I told you. They move fast in New York."

On his way to shoot some scenes, Dawson grabs the prosthetic "Joey" head before asking his father for some advice. Entering through Dawson's bedroom window, Joey overhears the entire exchange. Dawson needs kissing technique hints. Mr. Leery invites Dawson to practice on the prosthetic head. Moving in for the kiss, dad reminds son to close his eyes. An enraptured Joey does the same on the stairs. Her first kiss. In a manner of speaking.

Joey's death scene in Dawson's movie is incredibly realistic; her head is sliced off and she is covered in gore. Inside, changing into clean clothes, Jen tries to help her. But Joey feels self-conscious when Jen comments on Joey's "nice breasts." "Don't get the wrong idea," Jen hastily adds. "I am completely hetero. I am just commenting girl to girl that you have a nice body." Jen reveals she thinks of herself as a duck.

That night, Dawson decides he's going to the dance after all and Joey tags along. While she waits for party boy to get ready, she overhears Mrs. Leery make a tryst appointment with her lover, Bob. Joey confronts her and relates how her father cheated on her mother, who died of cancer. "Your actions affect others. They bleed into the lives of those around you."

Dawson's attempt to boldly cut in on Jen and Cliff goes awry, as Jen feels so embarrassed she leaves the party. Walking home Joey tells a crushed Dawson: "I don't understand how someone can be so self-aware and yet utterly clueless. It escapes me."

But seeing Jen lounging by the creek, Dawson asks Joey if he can catch up with her later as he wants to make a last ditch attempt with Jen. He professes that he does not want to be the friend that Jen confides her "boy adventures" to – he would rather *be* one of those adventures. To seal their new relationship status, Jen invites a beaming Dawson to dance. Neither notices Joey watching them from behind a tree. She has reluctantly accepted the inevitable. Or, so it seems.

Dawson to Joey:

"Jen is a mystery but I feel like I've known her all my life. It's like how I feel about you. She challenges me the way you do. She could be you – only she's Jen."

Episode Music

"Am I Cool" – Nowhere Blossoms
"Flames Of Truth" – Sarah Masen
"I Want You" – Savage Garden
"Happiness" – Abra Moore
"Pretty Strange" – The Autumns
"But You" – Paul Chiten
"You Don't Know Me" – Jann Arden

Kiss . . . . Episode #102

Teleplay written by Rob Thomas
Directed by Michael Uno

Dawson, Jen, Joey, and Pacey all stride toward their first proper kisses, but even they are unsure with whom they'll share the moment.

During movie night Dawson confides that he's waiting for the perfect moment to kiss Jen. Joey could not be more disinterested if she tried. She blames Dawson's chronic romanticism on the silver screen, especially movies like the one they're watching, *From Here To Eternity*, where

Anderson definitely has Joey's attention

Deborah Kerr kisses Burt Lancaster on the beach. "It's take 22, the girl's bored, the guy's gay. It's celluloid propaganda."

Despite her cool exterior, at the Ice House the next day, Joey fairly breaks her neck staring at a handsome stranger. Though she acts aloof, Joey likes Anderson as much as he likes her and goes boating with him. She lies from the outset, claiming she lives in New York, adding for good measure that her father is the CEO of a tampon company. On a deserted beach, Joey falls over during a game of frisbee, and Anderson falls astride her. He moves in for the kiss but at the last second Joey turns away.

Pacey to Tamara Jacobs:

"If you and I had gone to school together and we were the same age, would you have dated me?"

"Probably not."

At school, Pacey learns from Miss Jacobs that he's failing all his classes. He offers Miss Jacobs the chance to turn him around by becoming his private tutor. Testing Pacey after school, she is shocked at how much he's learned. The prospect of sex is great positive reinforcement. But Pacey's ego flags when Miss Jacobs rebuffs his sexual advances. "Find a girl your own age and not an insane middle-aged woman."

Filming the final scenes of his horror movie, Dawson takes Jen to "the ruins." The scene is filled with candles and soft music. Jen looks divine. Dawson shoots the last scene and approaches Jen. He moves in for the kiss but at the last moment, Jen realizes the camera is still on. She's horrified at Dawson's attempt

to record such an intimate moment. "You try too hard. You're overzealous." Dawson is overwhelmed with guilt and longing and insists his intentions are "never short of honorable." Hearing someone coming, they hide, but do not have time to remove the camera which is left rolling and captures Pacey and Tamara making love – unknown to Dawson and Jen. While they're hiding, Dawson and Jen realize the moment is perfect and share their first kiss.

Saying goodbye to Anderson, who is returning home with his parents, Joey continues her lies. Anderson gives her his telephone number and tenderly, they kiss – Joey's first kiss. Later, Joey realizes a comment she made exposes her lies and she quietly throws his telephone number away.

Episode Music

"First Time" – Billie Myers
"Kingdom" – The Slugs
"Too Many Times" – Wake Ooloo
"The Right Place" – Eddi Reader
"Pretty Deep" – Tonya Donnelly
"All I Want" – Toad the Wet Sprocket
"I'll Remember You" – Sophie Zelmani
"What Could Happen" – Meredith Brooks

Discovery .... Episode #103

Teleplay written by Jon Harmon Feldman
Directed by Steve Miner

Opposite: Miss Jacobs explains a little more than the intricacies of Shakespeare

Below: Pacey offers Dawson a lesson in sex and romance!

Though Dawson's an open-minded fellow, he never imagined he would one day film a risqué movie.

From the footage of the lovers' tryst at the ruins, Joey and Dawson can recognize Miss Jacobs, but not the young man she is romping with. Pacey is worried sick at the news the cassette exists and eagerly asks when he can view the tape. Joey assumes his keenness is based on his sexual proclivities

and quips he'll be treated to a personal screening so he may "flog his bishop in private." Pacey later confides to Dawson that he is with Tamara on the cassette.

With their twentieth wedding anniversary looming, Dawson's parents continue to maul each other like lovesick teens – something Dawson's incredibly uncomfortable about. He confesses to Joey: "I'm actually jealous of my parent's sex life." Joey asks: "You mean blondie's not giving you any?" In fact, when Dawson attempts to take things a little further than kissing with Jen, she discourages him saying they need not rush.

Dawson finally discovers his mother's infidelity – unbeknownst to her. He cannot fathom why she would do such a thing considering she is completely in love with his father. Ironically, he finds himself unable to talk to Jen so confides in Joey. Discovering she already knew of the affair, he rages off.

He returns to Jen, spouting the idealistic phrase, "secrets destroy." In an effort to make Dawson be a little more flexible in his opinion of people and

Pacey to Dawson:

"The Jen you have built up in your mind does not exist."

Dawson and Jen communicate without words in the pilot episode

perhaps to appease her own conscience, Jen reveals the real reason she was sent to Capeside. "The clichés you hear about teenagers in the big city are true. Growing up too fast, having sex too young." Innocent Dawson asks if her parents wanted to get Jen away from such kids. Jen responds that she *was* such kids. Including the sex part. Dawson's stunned. His silver screen image of Jen has been shattered. Dawson does not cope with the news very well and the next day Jen confronts him, claiming he has a "look" in his eye that was not there before.

With no one to turn to, Jen confides in Joey how Dawson has reacted to the news that she's not a virgin. Joey proves her worth by providing a shoulder for Jen to – if not cry on – at least feel sorry for herself on. Joey says, when it comes to Dawson and women "there are popes who have had more experience."

After failing to garner the courage to tell his father about his adulterous mother, Dawson can now understand why Joey was originally unable to tell him. Their first serious row over, they jovially point out each other's faults. Joey reckons he loses his temper at her too easily while Dawson thinks she's too critical. "Good night," Joey says, "All this subtext is making me tired."

Episode Music

"Beautiful Thing" – Kyf Brewer
"Top Of The Morning" – Hang-Ups
"I Know" – Barenaked Ladies
"Amnesia" – Toad the Wet Sprocket
"World Outside" – Devlins
"That's What Love Can Do" – Tom Snow
"Stand By Me" – Say-So
"Full Of Grace" – Sarah McLachlan

Hurricane .... Episode #104
Teleplay written by Kevin Williamson & Dana Baratta
Directed by Lou Antonio

If ever a weather pattern acted as a sympathetic background to emotional turmoil, this is it.

During movie night, Joey encourages Dawson to deal with his mom's affair with her co-anchor Bob at the TV station. Dawson quietly reminds his mother how wonderful his father is and she realizes her secret is out. With a storm approaching, Joey, her pregnant sister, Bessie, her boyfriend, Bodie, Jen, and her Grams stay at the Leerys. Grams disapproves of Bessie and her boyfriend, who asks her: "Which do you object to most, Mrs. Ryan, the fact that I'm black and she's white or that we're about to have a child in sin?" She replies: "What I object to is when children have children."

Dawson admits to Jen his confusion over his mother's affair: "I've got parents who bump like rabbits every day – you'd think that would be enough." When Jen tries to inform Dawson that sex is not always good, he insults her by saying she is more likely to understand adulterous behavior. "You'd better clarify yourself Dawson before I rip your head off!" an enraged Jen hisses before storming off. Feeling sorry for himself, it is up to Joey to remind him to be thankful he still even has a mother.

Dawson to Jen!

"Is the proposition of monogamy such a Jurassic notion?"

Preparing neighbors for an approaching storm, Pacey and his policeman brother Doug notice how frightened Miss Jacobs is by its approach. They offer to sit the storm out with her. Doug insults his brother one minute and flirts with

Tamara the next – completely unaware of their continuing affair. In private, Tamara tells a saddened Pacey: "You know we're going to have to end this, it's getting too dangerous."

Gale Leery confesses to her husband, Mitch, with Dawson in the room. Each time she comes home late, she says, she has been having sex with another man. It's been a lot of times. A lightning flash cuts the electricity and Mitch responds with an evasive "I knew I should've gotten some more batteries." Later on, though, he tells Gale he's chosen to stop loving her. "I choose to hate you."

In an effort to help him understand events, Jen reveals her history to an astounded Dawson, including her abuse of alcohol and loss of virginity at 12 years old. "I was sexualized way too young." It emerges that her father caught her having sex in his bed. "Daddy's little girl," Jen adds weeping, "fornicating right before his very eyes." This is the reason she was sent to Capeside. Dawson says his parents have given him hang-ups about sex. "They have this raging sex life and I used that as their measure of happiness." Jen tells him that's an incorrect assumption. Dawson apologizes to Jen and then Joey, promising he'll make every effort to be a friend "worthy" of her.

Episode Music

"It's The End Of The World As We Know It" – R.E.M.

"Healing Hands" – Mark Cohn

Baby . . . . Episode #105

Teleplay written by Jon Harmon Feldman
Story by Joanne Waters
Directed by Steve Miner

Though teen emotions fluctuate wildly, Dawson's unable to envisage himself with any other girlfriend than Jen and any other best friend than Joey.

Dawson and Joey's movie night is tinted with tension. Jen is there for the first time, uncomfortable on a hard-backed chair while Joey remains in her usual position on Dawson's bed. The poor guy cannot understand why Joey's uncomfortable. When she decides to leave, Jen departs also, citing her grandmother's suspicion as her defense.

Pacey and Dawson are overheard discussing Pacey's relationship with Miss Jacobs. This being high school, the rumor spreads like wildfire. Dawson tries to bolster his spirits by telling him: "You can control this," but Pacey doesn't buy it. "This is not the time for the Obi Wan moment." Ironically, it is Joey who is able to provide some comfort as with her background, she's used to hallway stares.

Miss Jacobs blames Pacey for the affair's exposure and she is rightfully worried about the consequences.

Returning home after school, Joey discovers her sister Bessie has managed to go into labor and get her truck stuck in a ditch all within the hour. They end up at Dawson's house with the only available help coming from the disapproving Mrs. Ryan. Spread-eagled and panting in the Leery den, Bessie is not pleased to see Jen's granny swooping in with orders for hot water and towels.

Doug to Pacey (ironically):

"There are actually people in this town who take you seriously!"

In Kiss (#102), Joey's a beauty, but remains naïve about the emotions this can stir in others

Bessie attempts to dismiss Mrs. Ryan as "a borderline racist who hates me and my boyfriend and my unborn child." But Mrs. Ryan simply gets on with the job, delivering a healthy and somewhat huge baby boy.

Capeside High School's board of governors calls an emergency meeting to discuss the affair rumors. Pacey can no longer speak to Tamara directly as all communication must be conducted through her sharp-suited lawyer. While Miss Jacobs is being questioned before the school board, Pacey interrupts to state the rumors are untrue. "Chalk them up to adolescent fantasy. Miss Jacobs is my English teacher and to my great disappointment, nothing else." Miss Jacobs is allowed to go free. Outside, Doug approaches her and says Pacey has always been "nothing but trouble." Tamara disagrees, praising Pacey as a "sweet, sensitive, intelligent young man," to Doug's utter confusion.

In their final parting scene, Pacey realizes Miss Jacobs is leaving town. "Us ending was inevitable," she says. "There was a ticking clock inherent to everything about us." Though Pacey is torn apart, it is obvious he will have nothing but pleasant memories about his affair.

Episode Music

"Sittin' On Top Of The World" – Amanda Marshall

"Insecuriousity" – Andrew Dorff

"All I Want" – Susanna Hoffs

"Seven Shades Of Blue" – Beth Nielsen Chapman

Detention . . . . Episode # 106
Teleplay written by Mike White
Directed by Allan Arkush

The gang and an interesting outsider use an opportunity to delve deep down into the true nature of their relationships.

During movie night, Joey sniffs at Dawson's personal belief that the romantic man gets the girl. "Guys are attracted to girls for totally superficial reasons. They like girls from New York with blonde hair, pouty lips, bony arms, and big boobs." After a thought-filled pause, Dawson replies: "Jen does not have bony arms."

The next day, Dawson flips when he discovers Pacey told Jen his childhood nickname, "Oompa Loompa." He later slams a basketball into Pacey's face earning himself a Saturday morning detention. Jen accomplishes same by using a swear word during a discussion on euthanasia. "This is not Times Square," the teacher frowns. "We don't use that kind of language here," which shows how much he knows. Joey's next to be sentenced after flattening a touchy-feely jock in the canteen.

On Saturday morning, everyone reports to the library. Dawson says "This is so *Breakfast Club*." As well as Joey, Jen, and Dawson there are two others: Pacey and Abby Morgan (Monica Keena). Their overseer for the day is the anally retentive teacher Mrs. Tringle, who recites detention rules and then asks: "Are you down with the program?"

Abby states her detention was earned for a drug-fuelled orgy. Despite her many, many faults, she does have a keen eye: "I think the four of you have some weird sexual tension deal going on." Complaining of boredom, Abby suggests playing Truth or Dare to pass the time. Pacey has to kiss Jen and then invites Joey to confess who she is in love with. Joey opts for the dare which – ironically – is to kiss Dawson, which she duly and somewhat delightedly does. To break the tension Dawson dares everyone to leave the room. He and Pacey end up playing basketball with the girls talking on the sideline.

Jen remarks how each attempt at friendship with Joey is rebuffed. "You could never be friends," Abby says, "as long as you keep fighting over the same guy.

Pacey to Abby Morgan:

"You're nothing but a white-bred, country club, goody-two-shoes with a bad case of potty mouth."

Joey, it's obvious you're in love with Dawson. That kiss was . . . intense!" Jen is stunned.

Dawson confronts Pacey and at the same time reveals his own insecurity. He feels Pacey would steal his girlfriend as he would "do anything for sex" and when Pacey uses his nickname, it stamps home that he is not a sexually experienced varsity athlete. Jen comforts Dawson by saying he is the only reason that she makes it through the bad days. But she is not ready to sleep with him.

Joey is the only person left without any resolution to her problems. She attempts to explain her own emotional turmoil but stops short realizing if she vocalizes her feelings, things will change forever.

Episode Music

"Stupid" – Chicken Pox
"Saturday" – Colony
"Alot Like You" – Colony
"Grace" – Michelle Malone
**"Will Tomorrow Ever Come" –
Dance Hall Crashers**

Boyfriend . . . . Episode #107
Teleplay written by Jon Harmon Feldman & Dana Baratta
Story by Charles Rosin & Karin Rosin
Directed by Michael Fields

Joey's eternal battle to make Dawson realize his romantic visions are a little out-dated continue apace.

During movie night, Dawson insists to an incredulous Joey that a man can be a "well intentioned geek" and still get the girl. Dawson's dad, Mitch, is not a geek and is having great difficulty coming to terms with his wife's infidelity. Thankfully though, he is still able to give Dawson good relationship

Pacey and his brother, Deputy Doug (#112)

advice: "Anyone who's never been hurt is either very lucky or very lonely. The trick is to get through it."

A leather-jacket-wearing, fast-car-driving cool guy from New York turns up in Capeside. Dawson is not amused when he discovers this is not only Jen's ex-boyfriend, but the boy she was caught romping with by her parents. The way Dawson's gaze flits between Jen and Billy, it's fairly obvious what is playing across the screen in his mind. Dawson is not amused when Jen asks if Billy can stay with him for a while. Nor can Dawson find any humor in Billy's semi-ironic boast that he's in town to try and win Jen back.

Joey's attempt to get the gossip on the situation is foiled by Pacey, who tells her: "You have some raging hormonal obsession for our friend Dawson and you just can't wait to get your hooks into him, can you?" Joey storms out. She later goes to a barbecue expecting a chance to speak to Dawson – but is denied the opportunity when he ditches her to speak to Jen. Billy turns up uninvited and the non-functioning *ménage à trois* begins to crumble. Billy yells: "Jen was with me long before she even entered into your fantasies," to which Dawson foolishly replies: "You and everyone else!" Jen is crushed and stalks off.

A piqued Joey, meanwhile, has allowed herself to be plied with alcohol and it is Pacey who extricates her from the octopus-like clutches of the boy who aims to take advantage of her. After Dawson and Pacey drop the drunk Joey home, Joey kisses Dawson passionately. Dawson later insists to Pacey she was probably dreaming of someone else. "My fine, oblivious friend," Pacey offers, "This girl is head in the clouds, 100 percent, ass-backwards in love with you." Dawson disagrees, claiming love is what he has with Jen, "new and exciting."

On his way home, Dawson spies a weeping Jen by the creek. She claims she needs to try life alone. "I'm sixteen, pretty, lucky, and fortunate and way too unhappy most of the time." Dawson is overwrought and teeters on the edge of begging. Good evening, heartache.

> **Joey to Dawson:** "Your problems really aren't that original. Divorce and dysfunction run rampant in this town."

Episode Music

"We'll Get Through" – The Slugs
"Being Right" – Cush
"Dammit" – Blink 182
"Elegantly Wasted" – INXS
"Green Apples" – Chantal Kreviazuk
"Evaporated" – Ben Folds Five

Road Trip .... Episode #108
Teleplay written by Rob Thomas
Directed by Steve Robman

Breaking up may well be hard to do but as Dawson discovers, it's the aftermath that's the truly painful part.

Dawson may be destitute but Joey is unforgiving. "A neighbor girl dumped you, no one died. Get over it."

Joey catches a lift to school from a jock named Warren, who then spreads the rumor that they had sex. Joey flames with rage. Her confrontation does not go according to plan. Warren reckons he has a reputation to live up to, while she has one to live down and insists the rumor is mutually beneficial. Joey, of course disagrees but is helpless.

Billy – who is long supposed to be in New York – returns for another attempt to win Jen back. She dismisses him and he then invites Dawson to an out-of-town bar. "Jen's a great girl, but the last time I checked, she wasn't the only one." Dawson decides he's going to cut school and be damned. Pacey hears about the trip and would not miss it for the world. Billy whispers to Jen and Joey he's taking the guys to a whorehouse. For once, Joey and Jen are united – if only in shock.

Joey to Jen:
"Dawson was the first decent guy you've gone out with and you've driven him straight into the arms of a prostitute."

It is Jen who concocts a cunning plan for revenge on Warren. Through the use of the school mouth – Abby Morgan – Joey spreads the rumor that she's pregnant. Though Abby soon discovers Joey's lying, she reveals to Jen that Warren "couldn't fertilize a garden." She adds: "He has a soft spot for the ladies . . . in a very unfortunate location." Joey uses the information as a bargaining tool, forcing Warren to retract his slur.

At the bar, it is only through the grace of God that Dawson manages to hit it off with Nina, a sexy, *Film Threat*-T-shirt-wearing film student. Ironically, Billy and Pacey are without partners for the evening, while Nina's prepared to take Dawson home. After Dawson explains he's still smitten with his ex-girlfriend, Nina says: "You've just restored my faith in the male sex." She's prepared to allow Dawson to sleep on her couch in order to achieve a reputation but Dawson decides against it.

Pacey does not always have a lot to smile about but when he does in Decisions *(#112) – it's worth it*

Back in the bar, Billy berates his lack of testosterone but Dawson saw through his plan from the outset. If Dawson had scored, Billy would have ratted to Jen – wrecking any chance of reconciliation. His not-so-cunning plan foiled, Billy drives off leaving Dawson and Pacey stranded.

Jen asks Joey if there's any chance they can stop Dawson from coming between them. Joey replies it should be no problem as he's only in love with one of them. Jen adds: "Must be a lot easier than just being the object of his infatuation." The girls try to imagine Dawson doing it with a prostitute but are unable to conjure the image.

Joey sits by Dawson's bedside as he sleeps. It is clear she is prepared to wait for as long as it takes.

Episode Music

"Truly, Madly, Deeply" – Savage Garden
"Touch, Peel & Stand" – Days of the New
"We Are The Supercool" – Space Monkeys
"Your Pleasure's Mine" – Super Deluxe
"Requiem" – The Slugs
"Carry Me" – Boom Hank
"I'm Not Sleeping" – Nowhere Blossoms
"Nashville" – Judge Nothing
"I Don't Want To Feel" – Sounder
"Monkey Mind" – Judge Nothing
"Right Today" – Swerve
"Thinking Out Loud" – Ron Sexsmith

The Scare . . . . Episode #109

Teleplay written by Mike White
Directed by Rodman Flender

Dawson can be relied upon to not let the superstitious date of Friday the 13th pass without fun and games.

Cliff Elliot finally persuades Jen to go on a date with him. The surprised guy then turns to Dawson for advice on how to entertain her. The cunning ex-boyfriend reckons the teenage séance at his house would be a good idea.

When Grams learns her little Jen is dating little Clifford Elliot (who even goes to church!) she's beside herself with glee. She never did like that Leery boy. Jen's uncomfortable with the idea of going to Dawson's on her first date but cannot pull out.

Buying groceries for the party, Pacey and Dawson stumble on a couple having a heated row. Pacey wants to intervene but Dawson says: "Domestic squabble, back off." The young woman, Ursula, ditches her boyfriend Eddie and ends up going back to the Leery house. Though the party of six – Dawson, Joey, Pacey, Jen, Cliff, and Ursula – are a little uneasy at first, things warm up quickly.

Ursula's in a world of her own making, with a loose tongue and a skill for scaring the others witless with horror stories. When the lights cut out, the party splits up to find the cause. Outside, Dawson and Ursula discuss her boyfriend. "Eddie's a monster. But he's my monster. You know, love's a really complicated bitch." Ursula says she can sense the vibe between Dawson and his girlfriend – the brunette. When Dawson corrects her, saying brunette Joey is his friend and blonde Jen is his ex-girlfriend, Ursula yells: "You're dating the wrong girl!"

When Ursula and Dawson return to the house, the others have concocted a plan to scare Dawson. Joey has gone missing and Dawson is the shocked one who finds her, gullet slashed open. Dawson's face at the sight of dead Joey says much. He is not amused when everyone starts laughing.

Joey to Dawson:

"Why do we need horror movies to remind us of how sick and demented the world really is?"

In private, Jen teases Dawson about his reaction and they're about to kiss when they hear a commotion.

Ursula's enraged boyfriend Eddie has followed them to the house and broken in. The gang manages to fight him off but Ursula opts to leave with her monster — the guys are too far out — even for her.

As Cliff escorts Jen home, she tells him she is not "in the market for a boyfriend right now" though she still gives him a good night kiss.

Episode Music

"Nobody Cares" – Vaporheads
"Will U Drive Me?" – The Rosenbergs
"Do You Dream?" – Mary Thornton
& Adam Castillo
"Temptation" – Tea Party

Joey and Dawson have perhaps their strangest conversation yet. Joey starts to tease Dawson about his reaction to finding her dead but realizes he was quite shook up. He reveals that it would be unthinkable were she to die. And Joey insists the opposite would be equally as unbearable. It's the closest they have come to verbally expressing their deep-seated love for one another.

Double Date . . . . Episode #110

Teleplay written by Jon Harmon Feldman
Directed by David Semel

In an attempt to make Dawson recognize that there's life after Jen, Joey is trying to prepare him for the inevitable: Jen's request that she still wants to be friends.

Dawson's carnival date, Mary-Beth, has an agenda of her own

Jen asks Dawson if they can remain friends despite everything. His concrete grin reveals how lost for an answer he is. Pacey advises Dawson to "feign indifference" to make Jen believe Dawson is not only over their

relationship – but is even starting to date again.

Why Pacey is dishing out advice when he's failing marine biology is beyond Joey – who has to join him to do an extra credit study on the mating habits of snails. Pacey is not enamored at being paired with Joey, who he refers to endearingly as "a repressed control freak." Left in charge of the snails for a night, Pacey manages to put two herbivores in with a carnivorous snail that promptly gobbles them up. He sheepishly admits trying to spice up the snails' sex life by attempting a *ménage à trois*. He's honestly apologetic though when he sees how important the project is to Joey and they decide to hunt for more snails.

Hunting for new snails, Pacey forgets to moor the rowing boat and he and Joey are forced to wade through freezing water. Once back at the truck, they change into blankets, Pacey managing to glimpse a semi-nude Joey – unbeknownst to her – in the rear-view mirror. (Warning! Objects in rear-view mirrors are more attractive than they normally appear.)

Despite claims of not needing a boyfriend, Jen plans a date with Cliff at a local carnival. Dawson invites himself along as proof of his indifference. His date is Mary-Beth, a super smart, bookish student. She's no fool and realizes it's a little too early for Dawson to be dating again but agrees to accompany him. When she spies Jen at the carnival, Mary-Beth says: "It's pretty obvious you're still hung up on her."

Pacey to Joey (who he has just kissed):

"If you kissed me back you would have been thinking about somebody else, right?"

Boys will be boys. Dawson and Cliff compete for female attention

Ironically, Mary-Beth has the hots for Cliff and grabs his arm as the foursome get set to ride the ferris wheel. Dawson and Jen are exceedingly uncomfortable and end up arguing about the reasons Jen broke with Dawson. On the verge of tears, Jen retracts her offer of friendship.

Back on solid ground, everyone goes their separate ways. Dawson bumps into Pacey and Joey who decided to come to the carnival. Pacey takes Dawson aside and confesses to new-found feelings for Joey. "I know you two have this long, tortured subtext. I don't want to step on any toes." Dawson insists that he's cool with the idea of his friends dating, then changes his mind and then changes it again, giving Pacey the nod. All the pondering proves pointless though, as Joey is NOT interested.

Later, a breathless Dawson finds Pacey to confess to not being cool with the idea. "You exhaust way too much energy on a girl you call a friend. Do you want the blonde or the brunette?" an exasperated Pacey asks.

Episode Music

"Baby Comeback" – Vaporheads
"What's Going On" – Lelsey King & Shelby Craft
"I'm The Only One" – Melissa Etheridge
"Hanging By A Thread" – Jann Arden
"She's The One" – World Party

Beauty Contest .... Episode #111
Teleplay written by Dana Baratta
Directed by Arvin Brown

Movie night can be educational as well as being a forum for the usual discussion on relationships. On the schedule tonight is a documentary about insect mating habits.

How do insects choose partners, Dawson wonders, considering they look identical? Joey reckons: "Twentieth-century men are conditioned to worship women who look like nutritionally deprived heroin addicts." Dawson counters with his belief that animal instincts also play a part. Joey rolls her eyes.

The upcoming Miss Windjammer Competition has aroused great interest in the gang – though not all positive. To Joey it's the "most archaic display of ageism, racism, and sexism known to man." But to Dawson, it's an opportunity to film a small news item for his mother's television station, and to tell Jen she should enter, classic beauty that she is. Jen instead says Joey should enter, the $5,000 prize money would be a great bonus to her college fund. Jen offers to coach and prepare her. "We don't have to like, wash each other's hair, do we?" a worried Joey asks.

Pacey to Dawson:

"Tell me the truth. Do you think I'm a tool for doing this?"
"I think you've got testicles of steel for doing this!"

Pacey decides to enter the competition partly for the money so he can leave home, and partly to humiliate his cop father. He cries sexual discrimination when the organizers attempt to deny him entry. When Dawson learns Joey is entering, he near wets himself laughing: "This is classic. This is so not you!" Seeing how hurt Joey is by his brutish comments, he apologizes.

Pacey shows Dawson how his attitudes toward Joey conflict. "You don't want her but you don't want anyone else to have her." Looking at a transformed Josephine Potter through the camera viewfinder, Dawson is transfixed. The gawky little girl from down the creek has changed. She is an elegantly turned-out, head-held-high beauty.

Pacey too has changed. Not into an elegantly turned-out, head-held-high beauty, but a charming young man nonetheless. Pacey's talent spot sees him paraphrasing the rousing speech scene from *Braveheart*. Joey's speech deals with prejudice and integrity, a quality other contestants lack. Though Joey does not win, she has accomplished much.

Dawson later confesses to her: "For the first time in my life, you've left me speechless. I feel like I'm seeing you for the first time tonight." Joey rightly sees through Dawson's momentary infatuation. "There's something not right about this," she says. "I want you to realize that what we have is so much more incredible than some passing physical attraction." Dawson's desperate to question her, but Joey's fatigued. "You've had a lifetime to process your feelings," she says bitterly.

The cherry on the pie is Jen's request for a reconciliation with Dawson. "Now is *really* not the best time," Dawson decides, more than a little piqued.

Below: Joey's voice proves as captivating to Dawson as her model look

Episode Music

"Small Town Trap" – Eve 6
"Girl With All The Good Boys" – Susan Sandberg
"Pretty Face" – Chicken Pox
"Fall From Grace" – Amanda Marshall
"Superman" – Goldfinger
"Surrounded" — Chantal Kreviazuk

*Dawson at the Miss
Windjammer
Competition*

Decisions .... Episode #112

Teleplay written by Mike White & Dana Baratta

Story by Jon Harmon Feldman

Directed by David Semel

Could Joey's attitude on movie night herald its demise?

Joey's had movie night up to her ever-rolling eyes. Dawson attempts to capture her waning interest with the cliff-hanger episode of a mini-series. "The producers put their characters in some contrived situation to make the audience think something will change but it never does," she sighs.

The next day Joey reveals she has the opportunity to study in Paris for a year. Jen thinks she should go. Dawson is more hesitant. Before she can go anywhere though, Joey has to visit her father "who art in prison." She and Dawson trek to the jail by bus and have to spend the night in a motel. Climbing into bed (fully clothed) Dawson's nervous as hell and stares at Joey's décolletage. Says he: "I can analyze someone else until the cows come home but as soon as I turn all that perception on myself, I lose the connection between my heart and my head. Does this make sense?" Exasperated, Joey counters: "What are you so *scared* of, Dawson?"

Joey to Dawson:

"We spend all our time analyzing our sad little adolescent lives. It doesn't get us anywhere. It's time to grow up. Everybody's the same. We watch a movie, find the appropriate life correlation then pat ourselves on the back. We need to move on — we're not kids."

Joey spends two minutes in her father's company; years of resentment spilling down her cheeks as tears. She storms out leaving Dawson to describe to the inconsolable Mr. Potter how wonderful his daughter is. Dawson later tells Joey she will have to confront her paternal resentment but Joey claims Paris is more attractive than Capeside, which holds nothing for her. It's Pacey who makes Joey understand she needs to confront her father and he drives her to see him.

Joey tearfully tells her dad that he messed up. "I'm fifteen and I go through every day thinking no one loves me." Joey's father insists not only does he love her, but Dawson loves her too. "Hasn't he ever told you? And you love him too. You have to tell him. Don't wait until it's too late." At this, Joey manages to tell her father that – despite everything – she loves him.

Jen's grandfather takes a turn for the worse in the hospital and she turns to Dawson for comfort. She spends the night with him but does not notice how distracted he is. In the morning, Joey rushes to find Dawson with an urgency denoting the message's importance – but spotting Jen lying next to him on his bed, she rushes off again. Jen returns home to find that her grandfather passed away.

When Dawson later finds Joey, he asks her: "Are you going to France?" Joey replies, all-knowingly, "Ah, the inevitable cliffhanger." Dawson insists he can grow up but Joey's response is: "I'm so tired of dancing around these big words. Are we ready to be honest?" And finally, they are.

Opposite: Dawson and Joey need few words to express their emotions

Episode Music

"What Do You Do?" – Dog's Eye View

"Angel" – Sarah McLachlan

"I'll Be" – Edwin McCain

"Broken Road" – Melodie Crittenden

"Say Goodnight" – Beth Nielsen Chapman

SEASON II

The Kiss .... Episode #201

Teleplay written by Jon Harmon Feldman

Directed by David Semel

If Joey and Dawson found being pals was often a trial, whatever will things be like if the friendship blossoms into romance?

Dawson and Joey's kiss is the culmination of months of angst. In other words, it's a scorcher! But shocked at this unexpected event, they almost decide to pretend it never happened. Dawson is not having it though and sweeps Joey into his arms for yet another smacker.

Ironically, while Dawson and Joey's relationship blossoms, Mitch and Gale ride stormy waves. Mitch will not rekindle their physical relationship and even goes to see a divorce lawyer. When Gale finds out he says: "I'm not sure I can stay married to a woman who I love and hate in equal measure."

Joey confides all to Bessie, who of course wants to know all the juicy details. Dawson confides all to Pacey, who of course wants to know all the juicy details. Dawson describes the kiss as: "The sweetest, most romantic, Fourth-of-July-fireworky, waves-crashing-against-the-shore, beyond-any-

Dawson:

"The hard part is over. We got through it. Fifteen years of preamble. Fifteen years of hyper-real dialogue disguising our most obvious feelings. It's all over now. The rest is simple. We'll make it simple."

movie-I-could-ever-imagine kiss." Pacey feels that if Dawson and Joey can get together, he can reinvent himself and shirk his loser moniker.

New girl in town Andie McPhee crashes into Pacey – who was driving his father's squad car – and mistakes him for an officer. Pacey milks the opportunity and humiliates Andie.

At school, Joey opts not to go to France. Dawson is ecstatic but Joey a little more cautious: "What happens if our reality doesn't live up to the dream?" Jen interrupts the couple to reveal her grandfather died. Overcome, she rushes off and Joey advises Dawson to check and make sure she's alright.

When she realizes Pacey's not an officer, Andie is enraged: "You are a real low life." But she realizes she can get back at him when Pacey reveals his infatuation with her cheerleader pal, Christy Livingstone. Andie introduces the two, but not before saying Pacey is dying of a heart condition and could pop off at any moment.

The last show at Capeside movie house, the Rialto, attracts the usual suspects, including Grams. Jen turns up unexpectedly and sits with Joey and Dawson, who are on their first real date. She leaves when she realizes her presence makes a crowd. Dawson yet again goes to see if she is alright and when he returns to his seat, he finds that Joey has gone.

Christy reveals to a humiliated Pacey the reason she agreed to a date. On meeting Andie at the grocery store, they agree they are now even and Andie even helps him choose the correct dye to change his hair color back to normal.

Dawson and Joey make up, and kiss to seal their relationship.

Episode Music:

"I Don't Want To Wait" – Paula Cole (Season 2 theme song)
"Say Goodnight" – Beth Nielsen Chapman
"Out Of My Head" – Fastball
"Birds Of A Feather" – Phish
"Swallow" – Nowhere Blossoms
"London Rain" – Heather Nova
"Have A Little Faith In Me" – John Hiatt

Crossroads .... Episode #202

Teleplay written by Dana Baratta
Directed by Dennie Gordon

The selfish, the silly, the simple, and the simply wicked all get together for a good old knees up.

Mitch and Gale are shocked to find Dawson and Joey making out heatedly on his bed. Next morning, the adults embarrass the duo with sex statistics and invitations to discuss emerging sexuality. Mortified, Dawson and Joey decline the offer.

Pacey fails his driving test – but Dawson, so smitten by Joey, forgets it's Pacey's birthday. Jen advises him to throw a party: "Forget Joey and Dawson, they forgot about you."

Confirmed troublemaker Abby Morgan shows an interest in Jen's New York experiences and they become friends. Jen shows the man-hungry Abby photos of guys she knew in New York. "I'd throw my mother off a bridge to go out with someone like that." Abby oozes. "How could you have possibly

Pacey to Dawson:

"Wait a second. Back up. You know everything about me? You know how I got this scar on my elbow? Or why my father hates me so much? Or the reason I walk a fine line between insecurity and supreme self-confidence?"

*Mitch gives a book
(rather than his wife)
all his attention*

wasted your time on Dawson Leery?" When Jen reveals she wants Dawson back, Abby comes up with a plan. "Every couple has its weakness. All we have to do is find it – divide – and conquer."

Dawson says to Joey the relationship should be easy as he knows her so well already. She disagrees. When she's out of the room, he spies her journal on the bed. Overcome by temptation, he reads a journal entry and realizes he doesn't know her as well as he thought.

"I'm so sick of Dawson and his stupid horror movie. I wish I could tell him how horrible it is. How stupid and putrid and rancid and flaccid…" Dawson quotes to a disinterested Pacey who explodes: "My God, I am so frigging tired of hearing about you and Joey and your boring little mini-dramas that I may rip my fingernails out for relief! Just get over yourself and deal."

Painfully, Pacey is alone at his own wharf party with no one but Andie paying him attention. They're both nervous and take comfort in teasing each other. Dawson realizes he forgot Pacey's birthday and apologizes profusely. Pacey says: "Everything is different now. You have Joey and our friendship can't compete with what you and Joey have. And I'm not the third wheel type."

When Joey realizes her boyfriend's intrusion, she flips: "God, Dawson, you invaded my privacy. How dare you. I could sue you for this!" Joey eventually forgives him after an age of apologies.

Mitch's friend Cole reckons if fidelity is the problem in Mitch and Gale's marriage, they should take the antiquated notion away and have an open marriage. Mitch proposes this to Gale whose dumbfounded expression reveals what she thinks of the notion.

Episode Music

"Sway" – Bic Runga

"Killers" – Feeding Like Butterflies

"Get Em Outta Here" – Sprung Monkey

"Always" – The Sterlings

"Kiss The Rain" – Billie Myers

"Luckiest Guy" – The Macananys

"Dear Mary" – Aryana

"Save Tonight" – Eagle Eye Cherry

Alternative Lifestyles . . . . Episode #203

Teleplay written by Mike White

Directed by David Semel

Dawson and Joey are not the only people mindful of the symbolic way Mitch knocks down the ladder outside his son's window.

In his wonderfully facetious manner, Dawson tells his father: "You can't handle the fact that the little boy you brought into the world has grown up – and that he's a sexual being." Despite Dawson's best effort, Mitch makes it clear he doesn't want Dawson and Joey alone, behind closed doors.

At school, economics teacher Mr. Maddock hands out an interesting assignment where the pupils study family economics. Pacey and Andie are lower-middle class, Dawson and Jen are loaded, while Joey's a successful single mom.

Abby encourages Jen to make a move on Dawson. "You're gonna spend the whole week one-on-one with him. So the question is – are you gonna be passive and masochistic and really irritate me? Or are you gonna be proactive and grab him by the dipstick and make me proud?"

Not much studying gets done. Jen works hard at lascivious eye contact. Pacey teases Andie so harshly about her family's wealth that she runs off crying. Joey rejects her sister's offer of help on the project and turns instead to Laura Westin, a single mom with a successful career. Laura's impressed with Joey's savvy and invites her for an internship.

Andie reveals her thoughts on schoolwork to Pacey: "You get behind one day – and then you're always struggling to catch up – you get more and more confused and then eventually, you end up on the street, drunk and dirty, wheeling a grocery cart."

Andie's brother Jack explains to a surprised Pacey that Andie does not have it as easy as he mistakenly thinks. The Saab and nice clothes are merely: "The last remains of a decaying dynasty." He hints at an unknown factor to the McPhee family history.

After a little studying in Dawson's bedroom, Jen declares herself exhausted: "I don't think I can even make it next door. Why don't I just crash here?" Dawson is wise to her game though and tells her so. "I know you're with Joey – and I accept it," Jen says, "I just don't respect it. And I don't mean this in a slutty, self-degrading way, but I just want you to know you have options. And I'm one of them." She scorches him with a kiss before departing.

Bessie confronts Joey, revealing how hurt she was that Joey did not ask for her help with the economics project. Completely overcome, Joey speaks from her heart: "I love you and Alexander and I never ever want you to feel like you're in this alone."

Project deadline and Andie has no partner and no project. She teeters on the edge of Mr. Maddock's patience, when Pacey rushes in with a thick binder of a project and a smile for Andie.

Walking through town, Pacey does not notice a woman watching him. Tamara, his former star-crossed lover, seems to be back in town.

Episode Music

"Anything You Say" – Chicken Pox
"Flagpole Sitta" – Harvey Danger
"Mary Be Mary" – Say-So
"Four Eyes" – Sozzi
"Swan Song" – Bruce Hornsby
"The Party's Over" – Catie Curtis
"Woo Hoo" – The Newsboys

Andie discovers not everyone — especially not Pacey — shares her enthusiasm for school

Pacey reminds Miss Jacobs how difficult closure can be

Tamara's Return .... Episode #204

Teleplay written by Mike White

Directed by Jesus Trevino

Even though Dawson's a confirmed horror movie fan, when things really go bump in the night, he gets going.

A romantic tryst with Joey by the creek proves arduous for Dawson with the cold, the bugs, and prickly bushes competing for Joey's attentions. Dawson tries to romance her with the natural beauty of their make-out scene but when nearby bushes rustle ominously, the couple flee.

The next morning, a surprised Dawson discovers Tamara is back in town, trying to sell Mitch a warehouse to convert into a restaurant. Swearing him to secrecy, Andie tells Dawson she's a little smitten by Pacey. Dawson manages to keep the secret for a few hours before telling Pacey.

To support Joey's interest in art, Dawson attends a lecture given by Laura Westin. He finds it "prolonged" while Joey finds it highly stimulating. Joey's tapped a hidden talent and reveals a real skill in Laura's art class. Viewing her sketches, Dawson is surprised and expresses his delight and satisfaction that Joey now has a hobby. Joey sees red: "Why is it that my interest in art is a hobby while your obsession with movies is a life passion?" Dawson is instantly penitent, but the damage has already been done.

Abby to Jen: "What is so great about Dawson Leery? He's just a guy with a motor mouth and a limp billy club. Turn over a rock and find another guy. The whole world's crawling with them."

Pacey's dumbfounded on spotting Tamara but handles the situation like an adult. He informs her that he's no longer a child and has grown up.

Jen and Abby meet a handsome fisherman named Vincent. Abby is brash and bold, but the quiet Vincent makes it clear it is Jen he likes. "I'm not interested in playing blue-collar pin-up to some oversexed, condescending teenybopper," he tells Abby. She then accuses Jen of stealing Vincent: "I saw the looks you were giving him. Batting your eyes at him with the mascara I bought you."

Joey takes Jack with her to an art exhibition and is stunned by his knowledge and interpretation – there are hidden depths to this guy. Dawson shows up and

Jen has her eye on someone

notices Joey withdraw. Later, he asks Joey: "What has changed between us?" She replies: "That's just the point, Dawson. Nothing's changed. You. Me. We're exactly the way we've always been. And I'm tired of it." Other than Dawson, Joey has nothing else in her life. "My entire life is attached to you." This is one problem which cannot be instantaneously resolved with a little psycho-speak.

Episode Music

"Harvest Moon" – Donna Lewis
"Breathe" – Colony
"Half As Good" – Zoe
"Northern Lad" – Tori Amos
"And On A Rainy Day" – Shawn Mullins
"Each Little Mystery" – Seven Mary Three

Full Moon Rising . . . . Episode #205
Teleplay written by Dana Baratta
Directed by David Semel

It's highly likely that Dawson and Joey realize that the moon is a symbol of chastity.

Gazing at an almost full moon, Dawson says he loves the romance attached to the satellite, but Joey reckons it bodes bad luck.
Abby is piqued when she learns that Jen is going on a date with the fisherman. "Old Vincent probably knows an easy lay when he sees one," she tells Jen, who slaps the taste out of Abby's mouth.

Gale is entertaining Gary Somers, an out-of-town reporter, when Mitch receives a visit from Tamara. He's overly gracious – arousing Gale's suspicions. It's not even Thursday night! Dawson spies on his parents and their guests, deciphering the subtext.

At the Ice House, Jack asks Joey why she's so angry all the time – she's too stunned to respond. He later kisses her and though she responds in kind momentarily, she then withdraws ashamed.

Andie agrees to a date with Pacey but insists he does not pick her up at her home. Pacey forgets and meets Jack and Andie's mom, Betsy. She invites Pacey to stay for dinner with her eldest son Tim and her husband. A distraught Andie rushes home and confesses that Tim died in a car accident, her mother had a nervous breakdown, and Mr. McPhee left. Andie and Jack have to deal with all this on their own and Pacey touchingly soothes her.

Abby to Dawson:
"Don't stress. Let them fight for a while, then they'll wise up, get a divorce and everything will be better."

Showing an admirable lack of shame, Abby climbs into Dawson's room to spy on Jen. She heard the Leerys' row and reveals things became better once her own parents divorced. Abby then makes a move on Dawson – not because she wants to but because she wants Jen to see them. Dawson escorts her out.

Jen and Vincent's date goes swimmingly. His ambition is to be a lawyer. They make out heatedly but when Jen attempts to stop things, Vincent declares: "What if I don't?" She responds: "I'm sixteen years old, Vincent. How's that going to look on your law school application?" He stops cold. Grams enters and tells him to get out in no uncertain terms. Grams later says: "I will not allow you to slide back into your reprehensible New York behavior." Jen is stunned.

Episode Music

"Catch The Moon" – Marc Jordan
"Secret Smile" – Semisonic
"Hands" – Jewel

A wise Dawson questions whether his parents are having an open marriage. When Mitch admits it was not a smart idea, Dawson says: "It doesn't take a degree in psychobabble to figure that one out, Dad." He begs his father to forgive Gale and Mitch is overcome. For the first time, Dawson has seen his father as an adult, frail and confused.

The Dance .... Episode # 206
Teleplay written by Jon Harmon Feldman
Directed by Lou Antonio

Dancing is supposed to be the vertical expression of a horizontal desire – but perhaps not where school dances are concerned.

Joey, Dawson, and Pacey do not share Andie's enthusiasm for the homecoming dance. The gang claim they'd rather watch a movie about something than take part in it. A smart Andie asks them if this also relates to sex, as dancing can be considered a form of foreplay. Strangely enough, the gang change their minds.

The upcoming school dance has three pals intrigued

Joey is worried about the way Abby and Jen have become friends. "Abby is not a good influence." To counter this, she suggests Dawson invite Jen to

Left: surely Andie never believed she and Pacey were merely sparring partners?

Opposite: a first kiss which will always be remembered

the dance with them and Dawson decides to try and hook Jen up with Jack. Pacey advises against it but the duo hit it off OK.

Mitch and Gale decide to have a trial separation. Dawson says to Joey: "…So Dad drove off and mom's crying over the kitchen sink and what I wouldn't give for both of them to be up to their old coffee-table antics."

Pacey refuses to dance all night, saying it is not for him. Andie's surprise on seeing him slow dance with cheerleader Christy Livingstone is easily understandable. Andie says: "We don't owe each other any explanations. We're just sparring partners. We don't mean anything more to each other than that." Pacey apologizes; he was acting on impulse. Andie forgives him and they share a tender first kiss.

Dawson to Joey:

"I thought *I* was what you wanted."

Jack and Joey have been avoiding each other since the kiss but finally have it out at the dance. He says: "I don't think you're angry at me for kissing you. I think you're angry at yourself for kissing me back." Unfortunately, a dumbfounded Dawson overhears and slugs Jack. Later, Joey tells Dawson: "It was a mistake, all right – a poor, poor error in judgement. But that's all it was, Dawson. And for you to blow this up into some earth-shattering scene of cinematic proportions…"

Dawson says: "Ever since we've been together, I feel like you've been pulling away. I thought this was what you wanted." Joey has been in such a state of worry over her future, she claims she does not know what she wants. "I got my dream. And now I don't feel like I have anything else. You have your future so perfectly planned. Everything you want to be and accomplish. But I have no idea who I am or what I'm supposed to be. And so I have to find my something."

Joey has realized that she has to be happy within herself before she can truly be happy with Dawson, the boy she has swooned over for more than a year. Dawson is again alone.

Episode Music

"Footloose" – Kenny Loggins

"Kiss Me" – Sixpence None the Richer

"Sell Out" – Reel Big Fish

"She's So High" – Tal Bachman

"Did You Ever Love Someone" – Jessica Simpson

"Special" – Garbage

"Take Me Home" – Donna Lewis

"Less Of Me" – Gramma Train

"If You Sleep" – Tal Bachman

"Cinnamon Waits" – Nowhere Blossoms

"Man On A Mast" – Wine Field

"Hold On To Me" – Cowboy Junkies

The All-Nighter .... Episode #207
Teleplay written by Greg Berlanti
Directed by David Semel

Proving how sensitive he is, Dawson has a quiet night indoors, sharing relationship chat with his mother.

A depressed Dawson and his morose mom comfort each other during movie night. She dishes out good advice about relationship break-ups: "See, Dawson, when you think about it, every inch of pain that touches you makes you a deeper, more real individual. Whether you're fifteen or . . . or slightly older."

Andie wants to try out her teen magazine's purity test on Pacey. She assumes his reluctance is because his purity level "would be closer to Big Bird's than Bill Clinton's."

Capeside High charmer Chris Wolfe flirts with Jen then invites the other students to study at his house. Matriarchal Andie struggles to organize everyone – especially as Chris tempts them with jacuzzis and satellite TV and, finally, Andie's own purity test. Joey reads out the poignant final question: "Have you ever been in love? If so, how many times? Give yourself a point of purity for each time." Her eyes catch Dawson's.

Chris and Jen score lowest on the test, Dawson and Joey score equally with 85 percent while Andie reveals herself to be 92 percent pure. Pacey's secret is finally out – he was foiled by the question about having sex with someone twice his age. Andie storms out embarrassed. He reveals that he slept with Tamara for sex only. Andie felt he was more sensitive than that but Pacey says: "I'm a sexual creature. And so are you. Why do you think we talk about it? Why do you think we joke about it? Why do we give each other tests to see how pure we are?"

Notorious womanizer Chris asks Dawson for advice to close the deal with Jen. Dawson's stunned Chris takes sex so lightly. Dawson later warns Jen that Chris has an agenda, but Jen saucily reveals she may have an agenda of her own.

Jen tells Joey she's sorry about her break-up, but Joey is incredulous. Jen then spits: "I used to think it was our mutual feelings for Dawson that kept us apart. I never considered the fact that maybe you were just a bitch."

Chris's little sister Dina reveals to a distraught Dawson that Joey wrote on her purity test that she had been in love twice. He confronts her: "You said I was your world. When did you have time for guy number two? I refuse to believe you're shallow enough to be in love with Jack after one kiss."

Joey wants things to return to a "pre-kiss" state but Dawson says: "Is that really what you want? After all we've been through – you just want things to be the way they were? If you don't see why that can't happen, if you don't get that – then you don't get me." Joey reveals she loved Dawson twice, once as a friend and once as her boyfriend.

After everyone has dozed off, Pacey proves himself to be a champion of last second studying and everyone manages to revise sufficiently. But there remains so much that each person has to learn.

Pacey to Andie:

"I swear those chick magazines are racier than *Playboy*. There's always some article about how to arouse your this or prolong your that…"

Episode Music

"Candy In The Sun" – Swirl 360
"Push Me Over" – Bob Mair
"You" – Switchfoot
"Losering" – Whiskeytown
"Nobody But Me" – Save Ferris
"Who Needs Sleep" – Barenaked Ladies

Mitch finds something to smile about

The Reluctant Hero .... Episode # 208

Teleplay written by Shelley Meals & Darin Goldberg
Directed by Joe Napolitano

Pacey teases Dawson for being a good boy, all the time, all year, all his life...

Pacey teases Dawson for being the last of a dying breed: "You take in stray animals. You help old ladies across the street. You just say no. You *are* Jimmy Stewart." Jen, on the other hand, has started drinking and it's Dawson who takes care of the inebriated girl when she stumbles home.

Mitch invites Dawson to his new bachelor pad. "I thought we could go for a bite. Hang out. Do like a 'friend' thing." Dawson's response? "Yeah, sure… whatever. I'll have to skip on the 'friend' thing though. Kinda have real friends for that."

An unenthusiastic guidance counselor, Mr. Milo, reviews Pacey's file and reveals he will have to redo his sophomore year. For once Pacey's too stunned to crack a joke.

Mitch to Dawson:

"In reality, people have flaws. I can be your father, Dawson, and…if you let me, your friend."

Hothead Andie later explodes at Milo's dismissal. "I happen to think you're one of the smartest, cleverest, most dynamic people I'll ever know." She takes it upon herself to save Pacey, to provide the encouragement his family does not. At her house, Pacey is stunned by the trophies in her room. "How do you do it all? I mean, I've heard of A-type personalities but my God, Andie. On top of everything, you take care of your family and still have time left over to try and rescue me? Aren't you — tired?" When Andie later gets a call from a local market where her mother has been causing a scene, Pacey proves himself a lifesaver and encourages the gibbering Mrs. McPhee to leave.

Dawson's horror movie won the Boston Junior Film Festival and the prize is 2500 dollars for his next project. Dawson wants Joey to produce again but she declines.

Speaking to Dawson, Jen is interrupted by Chris Wolfe. Even though he got her drunk at a party the night before, he wants to take her out again. Dawson's disapproving look sets her off and she insists — too vehemently — that she's having fun.

Pacey and Andie's joy is infectious

Dawson goes to the party with Jen and is shocked when he sees her being stripped by Chris and his friend Todd. He snatches her and carries her out. Jen slobbers: "You don't drink, you don't mess around with anything or anybody, yet you're the unhappiest boy I know." Dawson replies: "You're absolutely right. But I'd take my melancholy over your false happiness any day. Because it's real! I don't fight to pretend like I'm having a good time!"

Dawson takes her to his dad's apartment and apologizes for giving him a hard time, claiming he has always been a larger than life, Harrison Ford ideal. Mitch says: "No one can live up to that, Dawson, not even Harrison Ford. That image on the screen doesn't exist."

Episode Music

"Sitting With An Angel" – Dana Mase
"This Is Who I Am" – Shooter
"Hope" – R.E.M.
"Celebrity Skin" – Hole
"Got You (Where I Want You)" – Flys
"Acoustic #3" – Goo Goo Dolls

The Election .... Episode #209
Teleplay written by Darin Goldberg & Shelley Meals
Directed by Patrick Norris

With more than his fair share of insight, why does a script about teen love present Dawson with such problems?

Jen thinks Dawson's new script is "fluff," lacking teen empathy. "Innocence, sexual awakenings. Those things have taken a dramatic turn lately, both philosophically and culturally. Your scripts should reflect that." Claiming that Dawson was born an adult, Jen takes it upon herself to help him to regress to his teenage years. Says Dawson: "What's wrong with being mature for my age?" Jen's answer is: "Because it's going to trap you, Dawson. You're going to wake up one morning and realize the reason you're not growing is because you didn't allow for the process. There's a reason we go from infancy to old age. Think about it."

Andie wants to run for student council with Joey as her running mate. Unfortunately, Chris and Abby are also running and Abby's intent on finding dirt on her competition.

Dawson spies his parents in a clinch and assumes they're getting back together. Mitch instead says it was merely a mistake.

The election debate in front of a crowded auditorium is humiliating. Abby calls Joey a convict's daughter but does not stop there, revealing Andie's family history: the crash which killed her brother and her mother's mental illness. Distraught Andie runs out and it is Pacey's job to placate her.

Pacey to Andie:
"It's the nineties, everybody comes from a dysfunctional family. The only happy families are in TV syndication."

Dawson confesses to Jen that though he's mature, "Inside, I'm extremely my age emotionally. Maybe even younger. And my feelings are in direct conflict with my over-achieving, self-aware brain. And I'm sick of it. It's a constant battle. And I'm exhausted." After a skinny-dipping escapade, Dawson tries to kiss Jen but she withdraws as she has worked hard to win back his friendship.

In the office which houses the school loudspeaker, Pacey asks Abby why she wants to be *vice-president* to Chris Wolfe when she's obviously the brains of the operation. Unknown to her, smart Pacey switched on the loudspeaker and her vicious response is broadcast over the school.

When Dawson learns that his father served divorce papers on his mother, he goes to see Joey – but she is comforting Jack, humiliated after his family business was broadcast over the school. Dawson instead turns to Jen who fulfils Joey's role.

Andie, completely distraught at the turn of events, starts taking her prescribed medication again.

Episode Music

"Dead Yet" – Muddlehead
"Underwater" – Switchfoot
"Sacred" – Kelly Brock
"Amnesia" – Chumbawumba
"Slingshot" – Morely
"Troubled Mind" – Catie Curtis
"You Look So Fine" – Garbage
"Heart And Shoulder" – Heather Nova

High Risk Behavior .... Episode # 210
Teleplay written by Jenny Bicks
Directed by James Whitmore, Jr.

Dawson's script poses more problems.

Pacey offers Dawson advice on his script. "You write in too many syllables. And what's with all the psychobabble insight? How many teenagers do you know that really talk like that?" Pacey says it is obvious the characters are Dawson and Joey and that they should have sex in the movie. Dawson says it's edgier if they don't.

Jen has taken on another former role of Joey's – producer of Dawson's movie. As a result, she and Dawson are spending a lot of time together. Jen reveals to Abby that her new plan is to wait for Dawson. "Are you sure you're suited for the role of Joey Potter?" Abby asks. "Let me remind you that Joey's plan was fifteen years in the making. You're not getting any younger, Jen."

Jen tells Dawson he should think about rewriting the script: "Don't let it play out so real to your life. The way it is now this magic couple spend the entire film with this pent-up, secret longing that never gets paid off. There's no money shot. And I just learned that term." Dawson sticks with his belief that the story is stronger without sex: "The story will be stronger if they resist their lust."

When Jack spills a drink over Joey's art class sketch of a nude man, he offers to pose for her. She's hesitant but his persistence wins her over. As Jack reclines on the couch to be painted by Joey, it resembles the famous scene from *Titanic* – and Joey notices: "Except I'm Jack and you're Rose." Discussing sex, Jack reveals that it scares him, even though he's not a virgin. He describes his first time intimately to Joey using artistic metaphors and gets a little too excited. Once he calms down and gets dressed, he and Joey start to make out.

Andie wanted Pacey to get an HIV test – though he's negative, she makes it clear that they're not going to hop right into bed. She says she wants her first

Jen to Dawson:
"A true love story is fueled by lust. In reality, Dawson, sooner or later people who care that much end up having sex. Even people who don't care that much. This is 1998, sex is always risky."

In Sex, She Wrote
*(#211), Joey
tells Dawson she likes
the way he sees her —
so-o mysterious*

time to be special. Pacey then treats Andie to her fantasy evening — an intimate French restaurant and a bed-and-breakfast inn. Though she wants to do the deed, she's upset as she considers herself to be carrying so much baggage. There's a tender moment as Pacey confesses how Andie has helped him turn his life around.

A dozing Jen is surprised by a noise at her window. It is Dawson and he makes his intentions clear in the way he kisses her. Each couple moves tantalizingly close to the point of no return.

Episode Music

"Hey Now Now" – Swirl 360
"The World is New" – Save Ferris
"Please" – Chris Isaak
"Anything But Down" – Sheryl Crow
"Driving You Crazy" – Tia Tejada
"Lover Lay Down" – Dave Matthews Band

Sex, She Wrote . . . . Episode #211
Teleplay written by Mike White & Greg Berlanti
Directed by Nick Marck

Is Dawson altering art to imitate life or vice versa?

In response to last night's high jinks, Dawson alters his script. His character now does it with Jen's character. Chris finds a note about a sexual encounter and he and Abby embark on a search to find out who wrote it. Abby decides she will do the research as a project for Mr. Peterson's class.

Abby quickly points to the couples who are likely to have had sex: "Pacey's sexually experienced, as we all know, and Andie's fallen head over heels for him. Insanity runs in her family. Then there's Jack and Joey. They share that whole artistic vibe, you know, progressive, uninhibited, experimental. Then there's Dawson and Jen. He's on the rebound and God knows, she likes to bounce."

When Joey realizes the movie is about her relationship with Dawson, she asks to see a script. Dawson avoids the issue, but tells her he'd never say anything to hurt her. As part of Abby's plan Chris gives Joey a copy of the script.

Chris to Dawson:

"It's been so long since my own first venture into the jungles of love – I thought I'd ask a newcomer to the club. Was it hot? Was it steamy? Did your palms sweat?"

Dawson and Joey agree that they miss being friends

Abby riles Jen so much Jen spits that she did sleep with Dawson. On a mission now, Abby upsets Andie by telling her Pacey bragged about his clinch with her.

Abby then informs Dawson that Joey slept with Jack and gives him the nude picture Joey drew as evidence. "Jack McPhee drawn naked. Dawson Leery drawn ... out of the picture. After all those years you weren't Joey Potter's first. And you're certainly not going to be her last. I guess that makes you her ... nothing."

Abby's fancy denouement is spoiled by the fact that everyone is already arguing. Joey's furious Dawson's script is so transparently about her: "You're too busy rewriting your script to imitate life. I know all about you and Jen." It transpires the only sex which took place was between Pacey and Andie, but he was so thrown by an "A" he got in a test that he wants to slow things down. "I'm afraid because you're the most important thing to ever grace my life and ...and ... I'm falling hopelessly in love with you."

Before everyone flees from the room, Jen flips on Abby: "You're a lying, manipulative, cruel person and the fact that you're only sixteen years old makes me feel more sorry for you than any of the people in this room whose lives you seem so intent on destroying. You're pathetic."

Episode Music

"Human Beings" – Seal
"Life's A Bitch" – Shooter
"You Get What You Give" – New Radicals

To everyone's surprise, Abby fails to hand in her project and gets an "F" from Peterson.

Dawson and Joey make up as she confesses to missing their friendship. He responds in kind.

Uncharted Waters .... Episode #212
Teleplay written by Dana Baratta & Mike White
Directed by Scott Paulin

Dawson researches movie relationships when profound real ones are occurring right under his nose.

A classic male-bonding adventure – a weekend fishing trip – fills Pacey with dread. Dawson cannot understand why Pacey's nervous about the weekend as Mr. John Witter is a fun fellow. Unfortunately Mr. Witter alternates between ignoring and belittling his son. Pacey invites Jack along as a favor to Andie and forgets to tell Dawson, who is not too pleased.

With a sly tone Dawson tells Jack he's brave to leave Joey alone: "Because it's right about now that some new guy, some bumbling, naïve, artsy type could waltz in and steal her away."

John unthinkingly humiliates Pacey: "Simplest instructions in the world and you find any excuse for not following them. Why can't you take a cue from Dawson over there? He listens when he's being spoken to."

Abby to Andie:
"I'm the girl that everyone loves to hate."

That evening, John reveals himself to be a heavy drinker. As Pacey struggles to get his dad back to the boat, Mr. Witter passes out. It's only now Pacey can "speak" to his dad: "I'm here and I'm not perfect but can't you see how hard I'm trying? When did you give up on me ... when I was five?"

Dawson also has a moment with his dad, venting emotion over the

break-up. Mitch says: "I've tried to set a good example. To be someone that you can respect and look up to. But just know this, Dawson. Whatever your feelings are toward me right now doesn't affect the way I feel about you."

The next day Jack lands a huge fish but, unable to manage it, he leaves it to Pacey who excellently hauls it in. Even his father congratulates him – before spoiling it by telling him to enjoy his rare moment.

For production experience, Jen is following Gale as she works on a report on the buying power of teenage girls. Jen advises her to talk to articulate girls like Joey, Andie, and Abby. Taking a break while filming at Gale's house, Abby immediately invades Dawson's room. The girls find a porno movie and sit down to watch, shocked and amused.

When the interview resumes, Abby monopolizes the conversation. Gale eventually asks her to leave. Before she exits, Abby spits: "What kind of journalist are you? Oh, I know. A trampy one who sleeps around."

The girls claim their buying power is borne of insecurity. Andie reckons she's a fraud as despite being an 'A' student, her home life is a mess. "Every day I walk into school with this pit in my stomach. Because no matter how popular I become, deep down I'll always feel like an outsider, an impostor."

After they finish, Gale says privately to Joey she always wanted a daughter. "But then I realized I have you. You're my surrogate daughter, Joey. I've always felt that way. I'm so proud of the woman you've become."

Outside, Andie sees Abby has waited all night for her

Abby, Jen, Andie, and Joey find an intersting movie in Dawson's collection

Episode Music

"Heaved Away" – MacKeel
"Watch Your Step" – Matthew Ryan
"If I Had A Boat" – Lyle Lovett
"I'm Cool" – Reel Big Fish
"C'est La Vie" – B*witched
"Slowly I Turned" – Black Toast
"Ode To Stevie" – Black Toast
"Suburbia" – Moxie
"My Door" – Binge
"Bottoms Up" – Black Toast
"Peace In The Water" – Robyn Ragland
"Best Of Me" – Far Too Jones
"This Pain" – Adam Cohen

Pacey stands by while his father dotes on Dawson in Uncharted Waters *(#212)*

mother to collect her. In spite of her seemingly "normal" existence, Abby has problems like everyone else.

His Leading Lady .... Episode #213

Teleplay written by Shelley Meals & Darin Goldberg
Directed by David Semel

Dawson and Joey's first movie night since their break-up proves to be more difficult in practice than it seemed in theory.

Dawson interrupts Joey's art class to give her a rewrite of his script and notices the nude model. His embarrassment is quadrupled when the model, Devon, approaches him later, this time fully clothed. He asks her to browse the script and read for the role of Sammy. She's not enamored with the script and irritates Dawson by commenting on the overflowing angst. But her performance as she reads dialogue straight from an earlier Dawson-Joey conversation is amazing and she wins the role.

Andie's doctor is unwilling to refill her prescription claiming it's merely a crutch, not a cure. Andie hides her medication from Pacey but he finds out and confronts her. She insists she's alright and explains what happened at the doctor's office. But when she later loses her cool she insists she has too much on her plate. "Between my mother, school, Jack, and you, something's gotta give and the way I see it, there's only one expendable on that list." Pacey's stunned but refuses to give up on her.

Joey tells Jack she's completely OK with the movie but he's doubtful: "If I was trying to get over someone and get on with my life the last thing I would do is make a movie about it. Someone needs to tell Oliver Stone the war's over."

Devon to Dawson:
"All the angst, overanalyzing, and hesitancy to act on anything, I had to search my psyche and call back my adolescence."

A pensive Jen ponders school life in Uncharted Waters *(#212)*

In describing what it felt like to have his girlfriend kiss someone else, Dawson says to Chris: "It feels like your heart has been literally ripped out of your chest and stomped on, like you can't breathe."

Devon proves to be a troublemaker and says to Joey: "I see you lip-locked with the little puppy dog but clearly your heart is with Dawson. I guess this Jack guy is just a safety net." Joey flips, dismissing her as a "third-rate wannabe."

Joey approaches Dawson and confesses to finding the movie painful. "Isn't anything sacred with you? I know you're over us and everything we went through but did it occur to you that maybe I'm not?" He's incredulous and more than a little irritated. "I have a movie to shoot and I'm not going to stand here and listen to you bitch to me about what I've done. You left me! I haven't moved on!"

Jen's latest beau, Ty, invites her to a party which turns out to be a Bible Study group, much to her surprise.

Episode Music

**"The Four Seasons" (Winter) Op. 8,
Concerto #4 in F Minor, RV297 – Vivaldi
"It's All Been Done" – Barenaked Ladies
"Sad Eyes" – Bruce Springsteen**

Dawson later apologizes to Joey: "I thought that by making this autobiographically cathartic movie I could put the past behind me in one fell swoop. Turns out it doesn't work that way."

To Be Or Not To Be... .... Episode #214

Teleplay written by Greg Berlanti
Directed by Sandy Smolan

Advice that seemed to hit the mark can sometimes prove to be a bane.

Jack asks for Dawson's advice for a poetry writing assignment for the dreaded Mr. Peterson's class. Dawson advises him to listen to himself before putting pen to paper.

Pacey is doing excellently at school but has trouble with Mr. Peterson, who is a tad different than Miss Tamara Jacobs. Peterson forces a trembling and humiliated Jack to read his poem aloud. The ambiguous poem has homosexual overtones and Jack flees the classroom crying.

In study hall, Joey and Dawson overhear students discussing the incident, claiming: "McPhee's a total homo." Dawson says Joey should take such comments seriously. She disagrees saying: "You expect me to stand here while you try to give validity to some ridiculous rumor that Jack's gay?"

Pacey to Principal Markey and Mr. Peterson:

"Making a student cry, embarrassing him, stripping him of his dignity was not right. And while I respect this system, I do not respect people like you, Mr. Peterson. I don't."

Pacey asks Andie if she's ever contemplated Jack being gay. She hisses: "He's talked about women his whole life. He's crazy about Joey. He hates Madonna. He's not gay." When Joey asks Jack what happened he reveals the poem might (and might not have been) about his deceased brother Tim.

Next day, even though a derogatory comment was scrawled across his locker, Mr. Peterson forces Jack to continue reading his poem. Pacey intervenes: "What is it about you that gets off on tormenting your students?" He then spits on Mr. Peterson and is hauled before Principal Markey. She orders him to apologize, and because he refuses, suspends him for a week. Jack seems ungrateful: "I didn't need a hero," he says.

Andie apologizes to Jack for not being there to support him; she now realizes he's not as independent and strong as she thought.

Joey's in turmoil and says to Dawson, "Call me crazy but I thought once I stopped dating my best friend that I'd finally be spared the soapy, hyperanalytical melodrama of relationships." He offers great counsel and she pecks him on the cheek – their first kiss since the break-up.

When Joey musters the courage to ask Jack if he's gay, he says no. But over her shoulder as they hug, his eyes reveal this incident is not yet over.

Jen, meanwhile, has been having problems of her own. She reveals to Ty that his religion bothered her more than she let on. But Ty persists in asking her out and when she relents he takes her to a fabulous jazz bar and much to her surprise, even sups alcohol.

Episode Music

"Slide" – Goo Goo Dolls
"Know What You Mean" – Sister 7
"I Do" – Lisa Loeb
"Come Rain Or Come Shine" – Jennifer Kruscamp
"Walk Slow" – Chris Isaak
"In My Life" – Trina Hamlin
"Smoke" – Natalie Imbruglia
"Only Lonely" – Hootie & the Blowfish

...That Is The Question .... Episode #215
Teleplay written by Kevin Williamson & Greg Berlanti
Directed by Greg Prange

Inspiration to tackle difficult truths can come from a movie or a need to be honest to the ones you love.

Looking the worse for wear, Pacey has spent his suspension week watching movies in Dawson's bedroom. He has not spoken to Andie as she blames him for dragging another McPhee scandal to light.

To ease the tension between Joey and Jack, Dawson recommends they have a romantic meal. Joey prepares a slap-up dinner – only for Jack to cancel. His father has turned up – called by school counselor Mr. Milo. Joey then goes to a jazz club with Dawson, Ty, and Jen. While Ty is dazzling everyone with his piano skills, Dawson is sitting between Joey and Jen when his situation strikes him. "C'mon, here I am, single, sandwiched between two women who dumped me. I'm pathetic." Joey quips: "Hey, my boyfriend may be gay," and the three old friends laugh.

While dancing, Joey reveals she can read Dawson's emotions from his eyes. He gives her a heated look of love and asks her what his eyes are saying. She deliberately misinterprets it, saying, "I think what your eyes are saying is how comfortable it is for us to be here like this together... as friends."

Watching them dance, Ty wonders why Joey is with a "fruitfly" like Jack,

Jack to Joey:
"When I wrote that poem, it clicked something inside of me that has been quiet for so long. And it made me realize that whatever it is I'm going through is not going to go away."

instead of Dawson. Jen is shocked, claiming Jack is no fruitfly – but Ty says if it looks like a duck and quacks like a duck, then it's a duck. "You see," he continues, "the ducks want you to believe that it's not a choice. But the truth is, everything in life is a decision. All ducks choose to quack. And Jack is definitely a quacker." Jen is pleasantly surprised later when her grandmother reminds Ty it's not his place to judge.

The next morning, Jack makes it clear to Andie that they don't need dad to come home. When dad comes downstairs, Jack loses his temper at his cold attitude, and weeping, confesses he's gay. "I don't want to be going through this. But I am." Also weeping, Andie comforts Jack and tells her father to leave.

Pacey, plagued by a malicious Mr. Peterson, researches teachers' ethics at the library. His hard work pays off. Peterson was in violation of a long list of rules and Pacey, determined to see him apologize, has sent a copy to the school board. "I want this man publicly reprimanded for his behavior." But Peterson opts to retire early. "Did you really think I would appear before some collection of idiot parents and have them tell me what I've done wrong for the last thirty years? I'd rather eat dirt."

Jack finally admits to Joey that he's gay. "You've been such a good friend to me. Which is why I can't stand the thought of losing you. But I don't want to hurt you, either, so…"

Completely heartbroken, Joey's only comfort comes from Dawson, who wordlessly, gives her some solace.

Episode Music

"Tell Me" – Audra & Alayna
"Waterfall" – Din Pedals
"Calling You" – Jennifer Kruscamp
"Queen Bee" – Jennifer Kruscamp
"Sunday Kind Of Love" – Jennifer Kruscamp
"Where Are You Tonight" – Devlins
"Reckless" – Devlins
"Intimacy" – The Corrs
"Wait For The Way" – Beth Nielsen Chapman

Be Careful What You Wish For .... Episode #216
Teleplay written by Heidi Ferrer
Directed by David Semel

Sixteen candles prove to be quite a task for Dawson.

Pacing like an expectant father, Dawson's anxiety about hitting the big 16 is obvious. "I'm gonna be sixteen in just minutes and I'm still me. The same adolescent, whining, big-talking, little-doing loser I was a year ago." For the first time, Dawson expresses concern over the fact Joey dumped him for a gay guy and tells Pacey he aims to win her back.

Joey's preparations for Dawson's surprise party swing on Pacey taking Dawson out for the evening. Jack is attracting flies. Abby and two friends are ecstatic at meeting a real life gay person. Tracy says: "I just think it's so great that you came out and you're only sixteen years old. I totally watched *Ellen* through that whole tumultuous year, and she didn't come out till she was like, forty."

Dawson takes Joey aside and confesses that he wants her back: "I know it's still there between us. I felt it through the whole Jack saga and I feel it now. I know you feel it, too ... because we're soulmates, Joey. You and I are meant to be. Period. The end. Cue happy-ending music." Joey pushes pause on the happy music though by reminding him of the reason they originally split up – she needed time for herself.

His funk is still evident later on cruising town with Pacey and Andie. Andie's therapist had prescribed a night of letting loose to combat Andie's unhealthy desire to be perfect all the time – and Andie's letting it rip, insisting Pacey take

Dawson:

"I'm always trying to do the right thing, and look where it's gotten me. That's it isn't it? I'm too safe."

Abby and Jen try hard to have a good time in A Perfect Wedding (#218)

them all to a bar. Dawson and Andie get drunk before Pacey can drag them off to the surprise party.

Jen is stunned as Ty insists sex-before-marriage is not for him. He then adds that with her history it might be better if they split up.

Abby's attempts to seduce Jack, "I wish I could have nabbed you one sexual preference ago," are so successful that when Joey smuggles a drunken Dawson into his room to give him some coffee, Abby and Jack are caught making out as if their lives depended on it.

Dawson stumbles downstairs and launches into surely one of the top three embarrassing situations of his life. Presented with his cake, his wishes include mom not sleeping with her co-anchor, dad getting a job, and Joey finally, finally finding herself.

Joey visits Dawson later as he's lying in bed, sick as a dog. He touchingly confesses: "I'm so lonely, Joey. I've been so lonely… I'm sixteen and I'm so hopelessly lonely."

Psychic Friends .... Episode #217
Teleplay written by Dana Baratta
Directed by Patrick Norris

Any number of Dawson's favorite movies insist schooldays are the best days of your life – so why are this boy's so painful?

The new Capeside High lecturer, Nicole Kennedy, catches Dawson's interest with her knowledge of movies. On sabbatical from Hollywood, she's writing a script for a feature film.

The new English teacher turns out to be none other than Dawson's dad, Mitch. He's already told Miss Kennedy about Dawson's latest flick and movie-making ambitions. Dawson's reluctant to let her see the film just yet. Mitch's worries about Dawson being lonely are allayed when he insists he's busy with movie plans.

Joey and Jack are so cool around each other they're now able to check out guys together! A Frank is a horror (as in Stein) and a Leo is a babe (as in DiCaprio). At a local fair, a fortune teller, Madame Zenovich, tells Joey she must make decisions with her heart and watch out for a tall dark man. Lo and behold, Colin Manchester introduces himself as a photographer, more than impressed with Joey's visage. She's smitten – then discovers Colin's gay and interested in Jack. When Joey tells Jack he should date Colin, he freaks: "Why are you so anxious for me to go out with this guy – because we both happen to be gay? Just because there happens to be a second homosexual in Capeside I'm obligated to go out with him?"

Colin to Joey: "Sometimes I wish I hadn't been in such a hurry to move forward because at some point – it becomes impossible to go back."

Finally, Dawson lets Nicole watch his movie. Her words are not swathed in cotton as she dismisses it as a "preposterous soap opera about a bunch of teenagers who talk too much." Dawson teeters on the verge of tears. Outside, he sees Pacey and Andie, then Jack and Joey and has never felt so alone.

Madame Zenovich proves to be a ray of sunshine by telling Andie the pain in her past may not be the end of it. As if that was not enough, she proceeds to inform a disinterested Pacey that though he pretends to be confident, below the mask is a frightened boy. Pacey shrugs her appraisal off but is clearly disturbed.

In A Perfect Wedding *(#218), Andie confronts a merry Abby and Jen*

A hurt Dawson is exceedingly snappish to Joey who has realized he's hurting. When he explains how Nicole slaughtered his film, Joey offers great counsel: "You don't know her story Dawson. There's probably a reason she's living in Capeside and not in Malibu. For all we know, her big Hollywood movie could be the sequel to *Waterworld*." Despite the distance between them, it is obvious Joey and Dawson are able to comfort each other like no others.

Returning home, Joey meets the real stranger Madame Zenovich predicted: her father.

Episode Music

"Completely Pleased" – Semisonic
"Run Around" – Blues Traveller
"Angel In The Attic" – Debra Davis
"I Could Be The One" – Donna Lewis
"Life Is Sweet" – Natalie Merchant
"How" – Lisa Loeb

A Perfect Wedding . . . . Episode #218

Teleplay written by Mike White
Directed by Greg Prange

Despite Capeside's reputation for failed marriages, let it never be said the town does not appreciate a great wedding.

Still suffering from Nicole's blazing of his movie, Dawson reckons Gale's unable to give an honest opinion as she's severely biased. To top it off, the next day reveals his father is dating his least favorite film critic.

Joey's father, glad to be home, announces plans to help Bessie cater a wedding. Joey's scepticism is not dissolved by his assurance: "I'm the father, Joey.

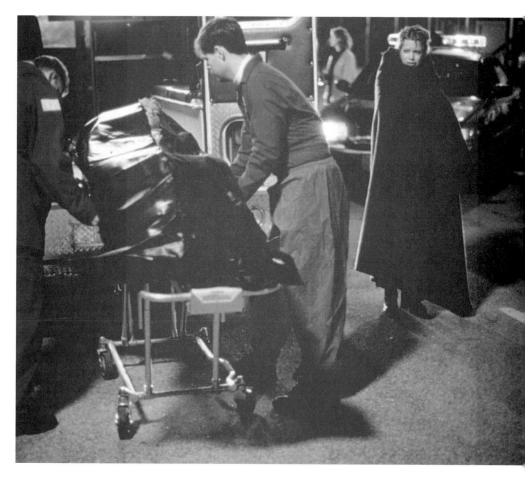

A shell-shocked Jen gazes as Abby is wheeled away

It's my job to worry. Your days of worrying are over." Joey asks her friends to help serve but confides her father-worries to Jack. "I can't just pick up where we left off."

Jen confesses to Abby she's bored and lonely, socially alienated from the other teens. Jen dislikes Abby – and tells her so – but admits Abby knows how to party. They decide to go to the wedding, ignoring the minor complications of a lack of invites.

Abby to Jen:
"I will never be happy. Wherever I am, I will always want to be somewhere else. Whatever I have, I'll always want something different."

The country-club wedding is a huge affair. On seeing Mitch walk in with Nicole, Dawson spills champagne over himself in shock. In the bathroom, he meets the jittery bride seriously over-dosing on second thoughts. Dawson's analytical skills fail to bring her round. But Jack, in under 20 seconds, reminds her of her love for the groom. She rushes down the aisle, leaving Dawson to praise Jack's emotional intuition. Dawson laments how Joey used to confide in him. Jack says: "There's no reason to be threatened by me. I may be her friend, but you're her soulmate."

Dawson doubts Joey's claim to be OK. She is worried about the Capeside's petty gossips but Dawson reminds her to be strong and accept her father fully. A mutually comforting hug indicates they're friends again.

Sharing a dance with Dawson, Joey tugs a heartstring: "Dawson, thank you. For being my friend. For understanding me better than anyone else. For putting up with me for the last sixteen years. I love you, Dawson." He responds with a kiss, and the entire wedding crowd are overcome with emotion.

Andie offers Jen some much-needed advice

Jen and Abby turn up half-drunk at the wedding, only to be escorted out by a strict Andie. Abby pilfers a bottle of bubbly and the duo make their way to the quayside to continue a dangerous drinking bout. Abby, giggling like a loon, bangs her head and falls into the water! Sober with shock, Jen dives into the cold, dark water but fails to retrieve her.

Abby Morgan, Rest In Peace .... Episode #219
Teleplay written by Mike White
Directed by David Semel

Capeside has seen the wedding; unfortunately, it's now time for the funeral.

Wedding emotions have thankfully twanged taut emotional strings between Dawson and Joey. The new couple discovers a wrecked Jen weeping in Dawson's room. She explains Abby's death. Her untimely demise raises issues for everyone, especially Andie and Joey who have lost people they were close to.

The next day, Andie resorts to platitudes which anger Jen to the point where she tells a mortified Andie it's her fault Abby's dead, after all, she threw the drunk duo out of the wedding in the first place.

Joey reveals there are issues she needs to confront regarding her own mother's death. "I know my mother's gone. I know that. But there's a part of me

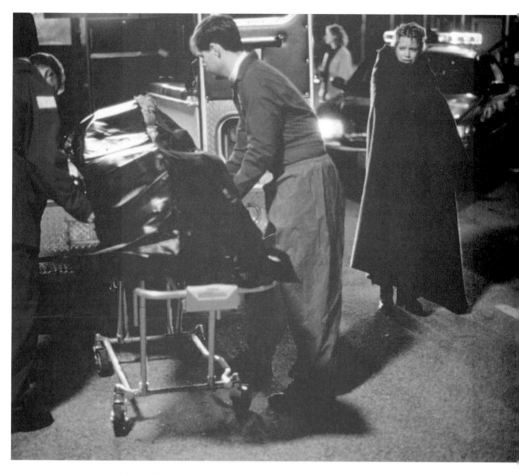

A shell-shocked Jen gazes as Abby is wheeled away

It's my job to worry. Your days of worrying are over." Joey asks her friends to help serve but confides her father-worries to Jack. "I can't just pick up where we left off."

Jen confesses to Abby she's bored and lonely, socially alienated from the other teens. Jen dislikes Abby – and tells her so – but admits Abby knows how to party. They decide to go to the wedding, ignoring the minor complications of a lack of invites.

Abby to Jen:
"I will never be happy. Wherever I am, I will always want to be somewhere else. Whatever I have, I'll always want something different."

The country-club wedding is a huge affair. On seeing Mitch walk in with Nicole, Dawson spills champagne over himself in shock. In the bathroom, he meets the jittery bride seriously over-dosing on second thoughts. Dawson's analytical skills fail to bring her round. But Jack, in under 20 seconds, reminds her of her love for the groom. She rushes down the aisle, leaving Dawson to praise Jack's emotional intuition. Dawson laments how Joey used to confide in him. Jack says: "There's no reason to be threatened by me. I may be her friend, but you're her soulmate."

Dawson doubts Joey's claim to be OK. She is worried about the Capeside's petty gossips but Dawson reminds her to be strong and accept her father fully. A mutually comforting hug indicates they're friends again.

Andie offers Jen some much-needed advice

Sharing a dance with Dawson, Joey tugs a heartstring: "Dawson, thank you. For being my friend. For understanding me better than anyone else. For putting up with me for the last sixteen years. I love you, Dawson." He responds with a kiss, and the entire wedding crowd are overcome with emotion.

Jen and Abby turn up half-drunk at the wedding, only to be escorted out by a strict Andie. Abby pilfers a bottle of bubbly and the duo make their way to the quayside to continue a dangerous drinking bout. Abby, giggling like a loon, bangs her head and falls into the water! Sober with shock, Jen dives into the cold, dark water but fails to retrieve her.

Abby Morgan, Rest In Peace .... Episode #219
Teleplay written by Mike White
Directed by David Semel

Capeside has seen the wedding; unfortunately, it's now time for the funeral.

Wedding emotions have thankfully twanged taut emotional strings between Dawson and Joey. The new couple discovers a wrecked Jen weeping in Dawson's room. She explains Abby's death. Her untimely demise raises issues for everyone, especially Andie and Joey who have lost people they were close to.

The next day, Andie resorts to platitudes which anger Jen to the point where she tells a mortified Andie it's her fault Abby's dead, after all, she threw the drunk duo out of the wedding in the first place.

Joey reveals there are issues she needs to confront regarding her own mother's death. "I know my mother's gone. I know that. But there's a part of me

– the little girl in me – that's still holding out, waiting for her return. Like her death was some cosmic error and eventually, God will realize He made a terrible mistake and bring her back to me like He did my dad – and I'll have my mother again. I know that sounds totally ridiculous."

Dawson has his problems to contend with unfortunately. Gale's been offered a job in Philadelphia and is considering it. She assumes Mitch would move back in rather than uproot Dawson in the middle of his schooling.

Andie is asked by Abby's misguided mother to do the eulogy at Abby's funeral – and agrees – much to Pacey's chagrin. He fears Abby's death has triggered something in his fragile girlfriend.

Andie to Jen:

"I'm a people-pleaser. I want everyone to like me and I want to make everybody happy. That's who I am."

Poor Grams almost has her head bitten off after trying to counsel Jen. "For the last time, there is no God, Grams. There is no Heaven. No peace. And no hope. The only truth I know is pain. So just keep your Sunday school fables to yourself. They make me want to puke."

Jen and Andie's eulogies are as different as the girls themselves. Jen says Abby had a "toxic personality" while Andie says Abby has made her into a stronger woman. Grams is particularly upset at Jen's comments and leaves with a face like thunder.

On her return home Jen discovers Grams has packed all her things and wants her out. "I went to that funeral to give you support, to try to rectify the damage in our fragile relationship, just to find you heartlessly thumbing your nose at me – in a house of God, no less." Jen turns up on Dawson's doorstep, a complete wreck.

Reunited .... Episode #220
Teleplay written by Greg Berlanti
Directed by Melanie Mayron

Capeside's most eloquent teens ponder recent events.

Dawson, Joey, Pacey, Jen, Andie, and Jack enjoy a movie together and toast an eventful year. To spice up their relationship, Dawson takes Joey to a fancy French restaurant but is displeased to find dad and vitriolic Nicole there. He snaps at Nicole who audaciously offers him an L.A. internship – after all – before she was dating his father she thought his work was weak.

Pacey:

"I think the important thing to be celebrating is not our surprising union but the fact we've all been through a year that would have sent the average sixteen-year-old off to the loony-bin."

There aren't too many fancy French restaurants in Capeside so when Gale treats Jen to a meal out, they end up at the same place. Jen and Joey concoct a plan to make Mr. and Mrs. Leery have a heart-to-heart. Joey deliciously embarrasses Nicole, who excuses herself to the bathroom. When the band not-so-subtley strike up a song which means a lot to Mitch and Gale, he cannot help but ask her for a dance. He uses the opportunity to argue a case for her not to go to Philadelphia, citing how difficult it would be for Dawson. "He's a big kid, Gale,

Abby's funeral brings
back painful memories
for Joey

and he takes after his father, he doesn't always know how to express himself. But I'm not sure how well he's gonna get along with you gone." Once the song ends, Mitch returns to Nicole's table. Walking home, Gale suggests she has decided to stay but when she spies Mitch kissing Nicole, the look in her eye suggests otherwise.

Poor Andie's pulse rate has been sky-high over impending finals. She has a panic attack and calms down only when she catches the eye of a handsome student who reveals his pearly whites to her. Andie's psychiatrist says she may need her medication again and the depth of her unease is revealed in the way she rebuffs Pacey. He overhears her talking to someone and thinks she was either on the phone or is having a breakdown.

Jack realizes she's talking to their dead brother but Andie is insistent: "I know what you think. And I'm telling you I'm not crazy. I'm not like Mom. I'm not like that. I see Tim. And he's here." She locks herself in a bathroom and it takes all

Pacey's persuasive skills to get her out safely, to make her choose him over the ghastly apparition that is Tim. "Andie, my life began when I met you. And you never gave up on me and I'm not gonna give up on you. I need you now more than ever. I'm begging you, please. God, Andie. Please. Choose me." Although Andie emerges shaken, the depth of Pacey's worry is etched on his face.

Ch – ch – ch – Changes . . . . Episode #221
Teleplay written by Dana Baratta
Directed by Lou Antonio

Movie night has a different spin to it this time. Why? Finals are in the air.

Dawson's working hard for a film class project for the dreaded Nicole Kennedy. He has to compare Humphrey Bogart's *Casablanca* character with a real-life person. Mr. McPhee turns up in a valiant but misdirected effort to help the family: he wants everyone to move back to Providence.

Pacey reveals his worry that Andie may be leaving. "Dawson, we both know that left to my own devices I'd probably be repeating tenth grade at best – living under a highway at worst." His pleas to Mr. McPhee fall on acutely deaf ears. It turns out Mr. McPhee would also like Jack to see someone about his "problem." It's no surprise Jack decides to stay in Capeside.

Mr. Potter agrees to be interviewed by Dawson but Joey's hurt by her dad's honesty: "Even if I could turn things around, would my daughters ever forgive me? How could they forget what I'd done to their mother?" When Mr. Potter leaves on an errand, Joey spits: "This whole Dawson Leery investigative-reporter-at-large thing is intrusive." She then tells him he should turn the camera on himself. But a troubled Dawson reveals his fear that he's one-dimensional: "A person who you'll one day grow beyond because you're changing so rapidly. A person that will one day lose Joey Potter."

Joey to Dawson:

"I love you, Dawson. So much."

"And I love you. More and more every day. And that's all I need right now."

Andie decides she wants to leave as Pacey is burdened by her illness. "He's already more worried about me than about his finals." Her departure is heartbreaking. Pacey's concern is etched on his face yet everyone knows this is the best thing for her.

Jen has called her parents to ask if she may return to New York and was stunned by their rejection. She packs to leave town – except she has nowhere to go. "I figured, screw them, right?" she tells Jack. "Why do I need them as my destination? If I want to leave Capeside, what's keeping me?" With his huge house empty, Jack offers the grateful Jen a place to stay.

When she catches up with him, Joey tells Dawson: "Life doesn't play out in three acts with huge character arcs and set-pieces and plot twists. Bad things happen all the time so when things are good you hold onto it for dear life." It's ironic she should say that as Dawson later spies Mr. Potter smuggling drugs, having graduated from marijuana to cocaine. Dawson faces a dilemma. Does he tell Joey the father he encouraged her to re-open her heart to has relapsed, or not?

Parental Discretion Advised .... Episode #222
Teleplay written by Greg Berlanti
Directed by Greg Prange

The things we do for love are sometimes, but not always, appreciated.

A troubled Dawson asks Joey if she'll always love him. She reassuringly tells him: "We get the happy ending."

Jack has to wonder if Jen is suicidal following her worrying comments about teen suicide and how she refuses her grandmother's plea to return home. Jen later reveals her depression by saying she is tired of being alone. Jack, as ever, gives good counsel: "I understand what you're going through, Jen. I know how numbing the pain is." There are people who care for her, he says, and is proved right when Grams accepts Jen – and Jack – into her home.

Pacey overhears his dad's radio reveal Capeside cops are observing Joey's dad. The sheriff tells Pacey to mind his own business and concentrate on his finals – or else. Pacey's so distant during his exam though, he writes nothing.

When Dawson next sees Mr. Potter, he says: "I don't belive that a man who claims to love his children with all his heart and soul would jeopardize their happiness by trafficking cocaine through the family business." Mr. Potter reckons it's too late.

That evening, outside the Ice House, where everyone has gathered to study, Mr. Witter breaks on Pacey for flunking his finals and slaps him. Shocked Pacey notices the Ice House is on fire. Inside, when Mr. Potter realizes, he rushes to flush his vile loot, leaving everyone – including his daughters and grandchild – to fend for themselves. It's Dawson who ensures Joey's safe before saving Mr. Potter, who himself became trapped.

In front of his deputies, Mr. Witter humiliates his son but Pacey pushes him away. As ever though, his dad's mouth gets the better of him: "Finally my boy gets a pair. And all it took was getting his heart broke by some little girl with a few screws loose." At this slander, Pacey punches the taste from his father's mouth: "Andie did more for my life in six months than you did in sixteen years, you rotten son of a bitch."

Suspicious Joey asks her dad about the fire. Mr. Potter swears: "As God is my witness, I have no idea." Dawson seeks his parents' advice; they order him to visit the police station but Dawson says: "It's about Joey. How can I do this to her?" Mitch and Gale insist Joey will understand. They realize their skill as a family unit and Mitch asks Gale to stay. She's willing to give the marriage another chance, but will still accept the Philly job.

When Dawson tells Joey – she blanches like a boiled lobster. Her father swore to her and Dawson has the cruel task of revealing his duplicity. Dawson asks her to go to the police but her temper flares: "He's my father, Dawson! I'm begging you, please! Stay out of it." Joey finally acquiesces. At the station, she's disgusted at the prospect of wearing a wire to entrap her father but realizes it's the only option.

Mr. Potter immediately confesses. Joey's heartbroken. "I trusted you. You lied, you ruined everything that Bessie and I have worked so hard for... We could

Joey to Dawson:

"See ya, Dawson."

"See ya, Joey."

have died in that fire, Dad. It would have been your fault." She reveals the wire and though at first shocked, he recognizes the wisdom in her actions.

Andie phones and speaks to Mr. Witter who seeks out Pacey to apologize for all that he has done and worse still, failed to do: "As little as I know about her…I know even less about you." He adds; "I'm sorry that I haven't been the kind of father you felt you could share your story with." Father and son share a hug to break a bear's heart.

Joey tells Dawson that she does not know if she will ever forgive him. "You see, Dawson, there are some circumstances that love can't overcome. From now on, I don't want to know you." Dawson was prepared for this eventuality but remains stunned: his face is a picture of utter, utter shock.

Who's Kissed Whom?

Incredibly, though the kisses are at times few and far between, **Dawson's Creek** has seen some pretty hot lip action. What matters though is that each kiss was based on honest and true, heartfelt emotions. Most of them anyway.

Dawson	Jen
	Joey – their second kiss was while Joey was inebriated: *Boyfriend* (#107)
	Nina – film buff in *Film Threat* T-shirt: *Road Trip* (#108)
Joey	Anderson – rich young tourist Joey romances: *Kiss* (#102)
	Dawson – the first time, most famously due to Abby Morgan's Truth or Dare game: *Detention* (#106)
	Pacey – after seeing her undressing after their snail trail, Pacey pecked her but Joey was uninterested: *Double Date* (#110)
	Jack – the first time – notoriously – while she was still Dawson's girlfriend: *Full Moon Rising* (#205)
Pacey	Joey: *Double Date* (#110)
	Jen – much to Dawson's anger: *Detention* (#106)
	Ms. Tamara Jacobs – this sassy teacher taught more than English Lit and more than how to kiss
	Andie – his first serious love affair

Dawson to Joey: "You and me. We cry sex until we're blue in the face, and when it comes down to it, it was just a few harmless kisses."

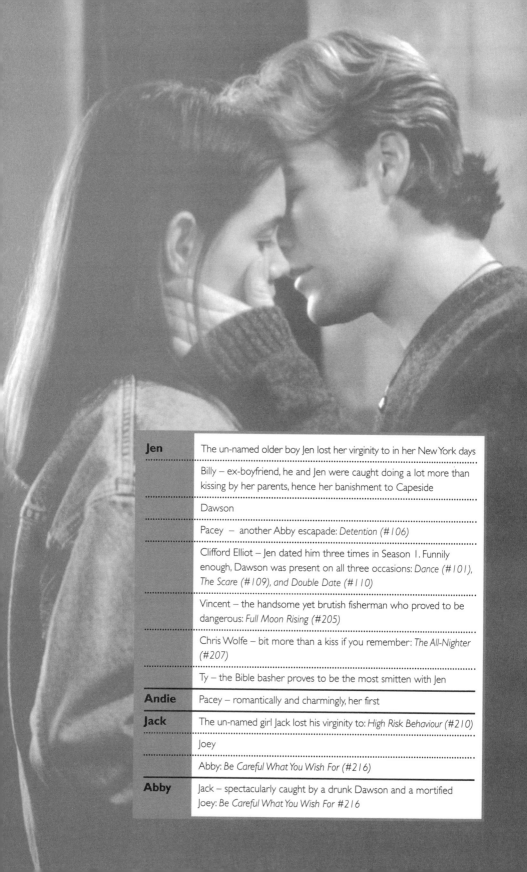

Jen	The un-named older boy Jen lost her virginity to in her New York days
	Billy – ex-boyfriend, he and Jen were caught doing a lot more than kissing by her parents, hence her banishment to Capeside
	Dawson
	Pacey – another Abby escapade: *Detention (#106)*
	Clifford Elliot – Jen dated him three times in Season 1. Funnily enough, Dawson was present on all three occasions: *Dance (#101)*, *The Scare (#109)*, and *Double Date (#110)*
	Vincent – the handsome yet brutish fisherman who proved to be dangerous: *Full Moon Rising (#205)*
	Chris Wolfe – bit more than a kiss if you remember: *The All-Nighter (#207)*
	Ty – the Bible basher proves to be the most smitten with Jen
Andie	Pacey – romantically and charmingly, her first
Jack	The un-named girl Jack lost his virginity to: *High Risk Behaviour (#210)*
	Joey
	Abby: *Be Careful What You Wish For (#216)*
Abby	Jack – spectacularly caught by a drunk Dawson and a mortified Joey: *Be Careful What You Wish For #216*

Fishing for Clues

Though we have seen how everything slots not-so-neatly together, it often takes time to work out Dawson's modus operandi. What is he thinking, confiding his feelings about Jen to an infatuated Joey? Why does Pacey aim his disparaging barbs at himself? What is with Jen's self-destructive behavior? But that is the key; in the same way retrospect enables us to see how events in our own lives slot together, it's only when we look back on each character's actions that we can see why the creek does not always flow smoothly.

DAWSON LEERY
Played by James Van Der Beek

If you want to know the trouble with being a self-aware, sensitive, and idealistic boy growing up in modern times, just ask Dawson Leery. A Spielberg lover, there are times when Dawson's face is a perfect replica of the "Spielberg expression" – an expression of utter surprise – you know the one where a character sees the shark, alien, dinosaur, or battlefield.

Dawson has seen none of those things but he has seen the fallout emotional bombshells often leave. Trouble is, as any 15-year-old knows, these are the kind of bombshells life throws at you every day. Dawson's calm, collected, highly strung, hopeful, smart, and sexy without knowing it.

And on the surface, his life is perfect to boot. We have yet to see the rest of the Leery house – that's how big it is. He lives in an idyllic fairytale landscape with trees, creeks, and friendly animals. Friends climb up a ladder into his bedroom. Most people who leave a ladder against a wall of their house are liable to come back and find everything – including the kitchen sink – winging its way to the local fence. For some reason, Dawson is oblivious to the danger that Joey could walk in on him "walking his dog." That kind of humiliation could put someone in therapy for a long while.

As an only kid, he's showered with the attention of doting parents. Half the marriages today end in divorce – but not Mitch and Gale Leery's. They are from the old school of relationships, married twenty years and still making out on the den coffee table – much to Dawson's horror. Mitch is a strong, smart dad with the physique of a wrestler. The kind of dad Dawson can talk to about

*Dawson Leery –
sensitive, self-aware,
and idealistic*

women – without squirming like a worm in the beak of a sparrow. Despite having great friends, when Dawson wants technique tips on kissing, who better to turn to than his dad? Although he pre-empts his question with a nonchalant "I don't want it to go to your head like I'm soliciting fatherly advice or anything…" this is precisely what he's doing. Dawson is not too proud to admit his inexperience and his dad duly trains him how to kiss on a prosthetic Joey head. Unbeknownst to them, the real Joey watches from the balcony.

Even later, when Dawson feels his father has not been living up to his expectations, Mitch proves to be a solid rock and says: "I'm sorry that I'm such a constant disappointment to you, son. I've tried to set a good example. To be someone that you can respect and look up to. But just know this, Dawson. Whatever your feelings are toward me right now doesn't affect the way I feel about you. I'll always believe in and support your dreams no matter how far reaching they may be. And you can always be one hundred percent sure of one thing. I love you, Dawson."

As if having a great dad were not enough, Dawson is also blessed with the kind of mom most adolescents would consider trading their own models in for: intelligent, articulate, ever-youthful. For heaven's sake, she's a news anchor! She wants for nothing and regularly and positively re-enforces Dawson's ambition to become a movie director. She makes great casseroles (even though they're a little too spicy), and never has Gale told Dawson to tidy his room. She accepts his best friend Joey as the daughter she never had and even manages to see beneath the veneer of trouble that Pacey wears.

The only thing Dawson needed to complete this picture of suburban bliss was a girlfriend. And while most adolescents have to hunt for partners in a forest of embarrassment and tentative approaches, Dawson has a beautiful, smart, sexy babe fall into his lap. In a manner of speaking. Jen comes from New York, the epicenter of sophistication, and – luck be a lady tonight – moves into the house next door.

Suddenly Dawson's bedroom becomes not only a haven but also the location for many a discussion on growing pains. Seemingly overnight, life becomes that much more difficult for Dawson to navigate his way through. All at once, Dawson is more than a little lost at the pace of change. That wry smile is oft replaced by a frown and never mind worrying about acne, he's already started work on worry lines. Can't a boy be 15 years old with non-divorced parents, a female best friend, and a blonde girlfriend living next door without the attendant hassle? Well, no. That is the sort of request "Oompa Loompa" would want, and that is the childhood nickname Dawson has long grown out of.

Dawson to Pacey:

"Think about it. Everyone I know is growing and moving forward but me. Joey's busy 'finding herself,' you've become the do-gooder, stable boyfriend, and Jen may not always move forward, but at least she keeps moving. My parents are starting new lives, and me, well, I'm no farther along than I was a year ago at this exact time."

Once Gale's affair is open news, it's like WWF in the Leery household. Except this fighting is a heck of a lot more realistic and the effect on a sensitive young man is all the more poignant. Though Dawson attempts to escape to his room as the fighting commences, he is still drawn into a living hell of whispered rows and fruitless attempts to articulate pain. Despite Abby Morgan's assertion that things get a lot better when your parents divorce, Dawson just wants mom and dad on the coffee table again.

Had Dawson been five years younger he would not have understood what "an affair" was. But at 15 years old and super smart to boot, he understands all too well and retreats to his room. The room is almost a character in itself. It's cluttered and tidy at the same time. There are *E.T.* dolls (a collector's item you know) and posters of Spielberg's movies. Like most teens, Dawson spends a lot of time in his room, the most special time being his movie nights with Joey, his lifelong best friend. Boys and girls are rarely best friends for life and the fact that Joey and Dawson have managed to accomplish this feat is testament to their great characters.

But unexpectedly, there are troubles in this relationship as well. Joey seems increasingly reluctant to spend time around Dawson even though he is the person she most likes to be with. What's going on? While Dawson would be happy to wrestle and romp on the bed for the television remote control, Joey's self-awareness makes her a little more careful about whom she sits astride. What's the problem? Though the answer – hormones – may seem simple, the solution is not. Joey endeavors, in her subtle way, to enlighten Dawson. She's a girl, he's a boy and besides, there's so much more of his genitalia now, what with his "long fingers" and everything.

But a key point to understanding this young man Dawson and how he thinks is that though he's super smart – with a vocabulary most university students cannot even lay a claim to – his emotional age is still that of a 15-year-old. He snaps (understandably) at his mother when he pressures her to confess her affair to his father. He then snaps at dad when he feels Mitch is not doing enough to save his marriage. Despite his psychology know-how, Dawson behaves like most other young men when Jen reveals to him the true way she lost her virginity and the real reason she moved to Capeside; he clams up. He's able to hug her and show support but his disappointment is revealed in the fading light in his eyes.

There are times when Dawson's reactions to emotional piques prove most destructive. After Jen's ex-boyfriend Billy has the audacity to tell Dawson he's in Capeside to try and win Jen back, Dawson lashes out. He insinuates she's been around the block quite a few times, hurting Jen to the point that she deems being alone is better than being with him. Oops.

He descends into the text book post-break-up melancholy, gazing out of his window, hugging himself. Joey has little patience with his moping and though she seems hard on him by telling him to get over it, we know that deep down inside, she's bubbling with anticipation. He is now free for her to take, although

Best friends enjoy the scenery and the company

When you're hanging around with not much to do, what better than to share a kiss?

as Jen so kindly reminds her, even when she's out of the way, Dawson still treats Joey as if she's just his pal from the wrong side of the creek.

In a painfully slow manner, things begin to dawn on Dawson. The reason it took so long? He only had eyes for Jen, he's a faithful guy and was completely smitten with the New York sophisticate. Even during detention, when Joey's dam of love almost burst, he was oblivious to her feelings. Despite the fact their Truth or Dare kiss was hotter than lava, Dawson's attention was taken fully with Jen's lengthy kiss with "stud" Pacey. Somebody kick this boy please.

It seemed that everyone but Dawson knew the deal with Joey, including his best friend, Pacey, who insisted she was "ass-backwards" in love with him. While Dawson is bathing in the light that Jen exudes, he cannot understand why he and Joey cannot remain the best friends they have been for as long as they can remember. Joey is more realistic perhaps. It may be possible to remain friends, but it's not going to be easy. She is prepared to simply sit and wait around, periodically tucking her hair behind her ears.

But then, seemingly from nowhere, they confront that boy-girl heat which simmers between them and kiss. It's a kiss they're almost ready to pretend never happened, but for once, Dawson acts impulsively and goes with his heart rather than his mind, opening himself to the first true love of his life.

At last. They're together. Unexpectedly, delightedly, and oh-so-rightly, together. It's spring and birds are singing, grass is growing and crickets are chirping or whatever it is they do. Dawson's buff in shorts. Joey actually smiles, bumptious in her cute little tops, her hair blowing freely in the wind. What could go wrong? Well, with Dawson, lots of things. He's used to being correct most of the time, and even by his own admission, he's a little selfish. But there is nothing more likely to rub Joey the wrong way than someone thinking they

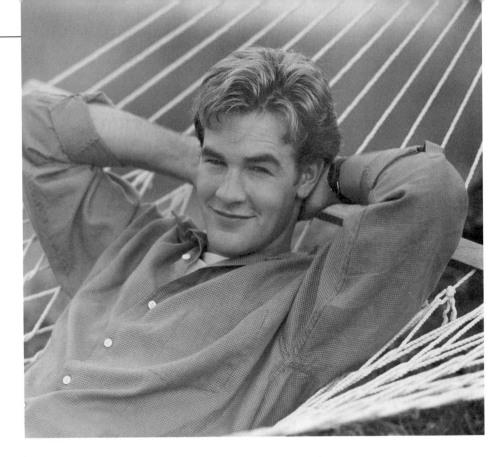

know her. She's a young woman who thinks. Hard. About everything. She's in the process of opening herself up emotionally to someone she has loved for a long time, only to have him smile wryly, open his mouth and promptly put his foot in it. "I mean, think about it Joey. Us. Together. It's perfect. There's none of that pretentious 'getting to know you' crap. I know everything there is to know about you." Oops.

Dawson's charm stems from his relaxed demeanor

By reading her journal, Dawson quickly learns otherwise. He is stunned. She may as well have kicked him where it hurts. With Dawson, his heart is where it hurts most. He's a sensitive soul, and to read that the one person whose opinion he values above all others considers his directorial efforts "flaccid" is almost too much to bear. She is right in insisting he invaded her privacy and though she actually forgives, we know she will not forget and will keep her journal better concealed in future.

The Journal Incident may have been forgiven, but it was certainly a contributing factor in Dawson and Joey's eventual split. They may both be just 15, and the relationship only weeks old but the love boat struck the major rock that most relationships encounter: boredom. Although he and Joey are still engaging in witty, verbose battles, they have been doing this since day one. Making out is certainly a new and delightful addition to their joint hobbies, made all the more tantalizing by Mitch's vain attempts to throw a wrench in the works. But overall, nothing much has changed. In fact, making out is the only new addition.

As ever though, Dawson is a little behind Joey in recognizing the symptoms of an ailment. If there was ever any doubt that girls mature quicker than boys, all one need do is observe Joey and Dawson. It's only when Joey's art – and Jack McPhee is certainly very artsy – begins to usurp her time with him, that Dawson recognizes her withdrawal.

Dawson loses Joey – not just because she kissed Jack – but also because she needs time to discover a circle of life which revolves around something other than Dawson Leery. Which is not very good news for Dawson Leery.

His new screenplay is an attempt at catharsis but simply makes it more painful for Joey to be near him. Thus, he not only loses Joey as a soulmate, but equally as painfully, he loses her as a friend. There are the civil nods in the school hallway but that's incomparable to the joyous movie nights they shared before. Dawson's head hangs low and the sight of Jack is enough to make him bristle. Dawson's efforts while he pores over his script are admirable yet pitiful all the same: all those words in his possession, yet he's unable to articulate his feelings, except through a script being acted out by an amateur actress, Devon, and a philandering jock, Chris Wolfe.

Slowly but surely, Joey warms to him once again. He's still hurting and would snatch her back from the thief Jack so quickly poor Joey would get friction burns, but her friendship is comfort enough right now. When it transpires Jack is gay, Dawson's response is fairly admirable. In the same way Joey was worried about what dating a gay guy said about her sexuality, Dawson could have been struck with horror that she turned him over for Jack. But no, at his level-headed, most-concerned best, Dawson puts others before himself and rather than concern himself with a perceived slight against his manhood, he is there to wordlessly comfort Joey when the truth emerges. Who wouldn't relish a friend like that?

When Dawson wins Joey back – and he does so in such a wonderful, calm, angst-free way that you wonder what all the stress was about – it's fair to say he has matured. Even though Joey accuses him of being a petulant child when he does not get his way, he's a determined young man now. Determined to do the right thing in love, in life, and in general. It is with typical Dawson irony then that it is Joey's father, who delightedly handed Joey over to dance with Dawson, who cruelly cuts short this waltz with his drug antics. Dawson does the right thing, he is mature, responsible, and adult. But Joey cannot deal with the consequences of his adult behavior and he loses her. The creek may look calm from a distance, but up close those waters are exceedingly choppy.

Joey Potter
Played by Katie Holmes

With the ease that comes from habit, Joey tucks her glossy brown hair behind her ears. It might seem like the carefree move of a girl without a care in the world, but we know Joey well and know she does not fit that description at all. Without a doubt, Joey has the heaviest burden of all the characters to carry. Despite past problems – or perhaps because of them – Joey is a headstrong, vibrant, wily, sultry, and determined go-getter. And yet, in a gloriously contradictory manner, in spite of her tough-as-nails exterior demeanor, Joey's also a frail, sometimes uncertain, emotionally sensitive, in-need-of-love person. And it is this contrast — hard, yet soft — which makes her such an endearing personality.

How is it even possible that Dawson and Joey are friends? The contrast between their home lives could not be sharper. It's frankly astounding she and Dawson have remained friends as long as they have. But, truth is, it's precisely because of their differing home lives that they have steadfastly stuck by each other for so long. Dawson and Joey each provide the other with the emotional back-up they may not receive at home. Dawson gives Joey a warmth and open affection she receives nowhere else. Joey, meanwhile, provides Dawson with a constant — and sometimes necessarily harsh — reality check. After a particularly humiliating moment for Dawson, when his attempt to cut in on Jen and Cliff Elliott's dance fails, Joey's there to remind him, tongue firmly in cheek, that they should stay in and watch movies on a Saturday night.

Joey to Dawson: "We should always stay home on a Saturday night and watch movies because the rewind on the remote of life does not work."

We can all sympathize with Joey's life history and comprehend how her character has been shaped by events. At only 15 years old, Joey has already nursed her mother, Lillian, who died of breast cancer. During this time, Joey also had to deal with the knowledge that her father Mike had been unfaithful to her mother. Joey believes the stress and strain of her mother's dysfunctional family life did not ease her pain. Unknown to Dawson, Joey bravely confronts his mother Gale when she discovers she is having an affair. Ironically, Joey is loath to deal with her father about the same issues. But following the advice of Dawson and Pacey, she thankfully realizes this is an important step for her.

For Joey, adolescence is proving particularly angst-ridden. Adolescence is the time in life when many people are struggling hard to find themselves and Joey is struggling like a trooper. She's finding out the nature of her friendships, relationships, and her place in the big wheel. Though she's never vocalized it, Joey feels her parents have betrayed her. Theoretically, they have left her an orphan. Coupled with this, she has to deal with the fact that the friend whose bed she's innocently slept in for much of her life has become so much more to her. No more sleepovers.

One of the first things we hear from Joey, which shows she's aware of the games teen emotions can play, is her warning to Dawson: "I just think our emerging hormones are destined to alter our relationship and I'm trying to limit the fallout." But being aware of something and being able to affect its consequences are two different things. And Joey learns this — like everyone else does — the hard way.

Unfortunately, Dawson does not realize there's a lesson to be learned and so he's not signed up for the class. Joey proves what we've known for years; girls mature a lot faster than boys do. Dawson does not understand what Joey's babbling about. What do hormones have to do with the latest horror movie? Gloriously unaware, Dawson reduces Joey to the status of pal, buddy, one of the guys he can have a laugh with.

Joey has come to the conclusion that the best way in which to protect herself from further emotional hurt is to keep everyone at arm's length. And if possible, a little further away. The tools in her armory to accomplish this

Opposite: Katie Holmes as Joey Potter

include the sharpest and quickest tongue in town. This normally succeeds in keeping unwelcome types away, but fails with those too stupid to comprehend her caustic put-downs. When Grant, an imbecile jock at Capeside High, makes an unsophisticated pass at Joey, she resorts to another weapon: her fists. Looking uncannily like Lara Croft from *Tomb Raider*, Joey deftly knees him where it hurts a boy most.

It's Joey's quick wit though that puts her in direct conflict with the other fast-talker in town. Joey and Pacey verbally bash each other until they reach a simmering pact of peace. Why the truce? Well, Joey thawed a little. She eventually accepts that the threesome – herself, Pacey, and, sigh, Dawson – has now become a foursome with the entrance of Jen. Not only that, Joey now has to deal with the fact that not only is Dawson dating Jen, but he's also absolutely smitten with her. And of course, being Dawson Leery, he's constantly describing his feelings. And teeth clamped firmly together, Joey sits and listens to his verbose descriptions of his feelings. Is it any wonder she rolls her eyes and snaps at anything that moves? It's a wonder she did not spontaneously combust when Dawson, concerned about his kissing technique, ended up practicing on a prosthetic "Joey" head he created for his movie.

Joey shares a rare moment of girl talk with Jen, who has split from Dawson, and reveals how her status as his "friend" makes her feel: "Dawson will always see me as the gawky little girl down the creek." Ironically, the role Dawson does not want to play with Jen – being a friend she can tell all her love adventures to – he unknowingly forces Joey to play. And playing that role with Dawson as your opposite is murder. Dawson is unlike most guys, remember. Man, oh man can he talk! He agonizes and theorizes and ruminates constantly. Is it any wonder Joey has a severe case of eye-rolling-itis?

It has to be said that Joey was a bitch to Jen. We know the little missy came in from out of town and snatched a naïve Dawson from under Joey's nose but in Jen's defense, she was not to know! Jen inquired about the nature of Dawson and Joey's relationship and he was so quick to cite Joey as a platonic friend it's amazing Jen didn't have whiplash. Joey had every right to behave as she did, and recoil whenever Jen made attempts to be girlfriends. Jen innocently says: "Hey, Joey, I love your lipstick. What shade is that?" And what is Joey's whip-quick response? "Wicked red. I love your hair color. What number is that?" Mean, just mean.

Joey's release from tension comes the moment she concludes Dawson will not be hers. The vicious cycle of wanting and not being able to have is broken. She still wants him, but is able to start coping with the fact that she will not get him. The visible parts of the iceberg reduced, Joey's infatuation was not so apparent any more.

And then, when he sees Joey in a new light in the Miss Windjammer contest, Dawson reciprocates! It's fantastic and about time too! Their kiss melts the icebergs completely and leaves room in her heart for everyone, including Jen. Even when Jen started wearing the type of dresses to homework sessions with Dawson that an actress would think thrice about wearing to the Oscars.

And even though Dawson and Joey's affair is short-lived, Dawson is worth it. The changes Dawson brings in her are astounding. Her art explodes with emotion. Dawson is the type of first proper boyfriend every girl deserves: attentive, honest, caring.

For Dawson, Joey turns down the opportunity to go to France. This would have given her the opportunity to reinvent herself, the same way Capeside offered fresh chances to Jen. "I wouldn't be Joey, the waitress," she says. "Or Joey, the daughter of a convict. Or Joey, the white trash girl on the creek. Or Joey, half of the 'will they or won't they' couple of the century."

But as brave as Joey is in allowing herself to be swept upon the emotional tide of Dawson, she has to be equally commended for clambering ashore. Her only desires in life were to get Dawson and study hard to escape Capeside. But what comes afterward? Joey knows not. And with one illicit kiss, Jack showed her that, shock and horror, there were other boys besides Dawson

*Joey gets ready for an
important date*

Leery! Which was not good news for Dawson Leery.

Jack is delicious to Joey. He is, as Abby astutely recognizes, artsy and bohemian and experimental. He poses nude knowing how important it is for Joey – her need for a model that is – not her need to see a naked man. He shows her she can be loved wholeheartedly by someone new, someone she has not known her all her life.

But he's gay. Joey's devastated when he admits the truth. It forces her to take a look at herself, at her own sexuality. Perhaps she is so cold, she was considered a safe choice for Jack? She is heartbroken and humiliated and rightly so. But the proof of how warm-hearted Joey is comes when, after all her pain, after falling into Dawson's arms sobbing to the point of dehydration, she's able to forgive Jack and remain his friend. She and Jack can even check out boys in the lunch line. When Jack feels low and fears being dismissed as the Ellen of Capeside, it's Joey who offers him the best counsel: "Don't you know that every teenager, probably every person, feels alone and wants to feel normal, but I'm not sure if anyone ever does." And Joey is, after all, another teen struggling seemingly alone through her wonder years.

And now Joey has to try and rescue her friendship with Dawson. He's attempting to work through his problems with a cathartic movie but that does not work for her. Joey reveals maturity beyond her years with her ability to confront difficult issues. Despite all the pain Dawson's feeling, and the noisome heartache she's wading through, she's able to articulate the true reasons she split up with him, revealing that it was never solely about Jack. "It was never about looking for something better. It was about looking for someone that wasn't so close to me, that I could tell where I ended and he began. Our lives have been so intertwined…in many ways, you partially invented me. That scares me so much, sometimes. I need to find out if I'm capable of being a whole person without you."

The moment Dawson understands Joey's on a personal quest, he can reclaim the friendship they both rely upon so much. He is able to alleviate Joey's abandonment fears when her father returns and encourages her to accept his return. And ironically, it is her father who returns the favor by literally handing her over to Dawson for a dance, a kiss, and more.

But as Joey probably curses herself, can her happiness ever be anything but ephemeral? Joey once again gets trapped in Daddy's web of self-destruction, but more pointedly, Dawson knew the sticky entanglement was there but was unable to help her avoid it. A break-up with your true love is hard on the heart and Joey's is fragile to begin with. She only hopes that it can be repaired. How many break-ups and make-ups can she survive?

PACEY WITTER
Played by Joshua Jackson

To us, Pacey Witter is a young man after many a boisterous young teen's heart. To other people, he's different things. He's the lil' devil on the left shoulder telling them to follow their emotions and be damned, take dad's car and go for a cruise. Dawson by contrast is clad in white ruminating on the emotional and calorie ramifications of having another chocolate cookie. Thank goodness there's someone on the creek who will take an illicit day off school without handing in their math homework first. Pacey understands that forgiveness is sometimes easier to obtain than permission and operates accordingly. Pacey is rebellious, rambunctious, horny, hearty, fun, and faithful.

Thankfully, he's also a resilient guy. It's confounding he can remain as optimistic as he is despite his home life, one that would have crushed the spirit of lesser mortals like a tin can in a car crusher. His father, John Witter, Capeside's chief of police, bears down on him as if he's the most wanted in town instead of his son. If only Pacey had an elder brother to stick up for him. Instead, he's lumbered with Deputy Doug, who, anxious to please his father or simply knowing no better, joins in the favorite family pastime of criticizing Pacey's every movement. To these two men, who in any functional family would be the source of great inspiration and support to a young man, Pacey is a bane. He does not live up to their standards, carry the Witter family name with pride or show any intention of wearing the badges they sport with heads held high.

At one stage, Pacey probably would not have made the grade to become a policeman. This was not because he was unintelligent, but because he had resigned himself to being the fool his family already cast him as being. Why try to win the game when the results are already fixed? But that was before The Change.

The trouble with Pacey is, he presents himself as different things to different people. To his family he presents himself as an incompetent. He plays the fool to them, hides his intelligence, and quips continually to put on the front that their verbal barbs are painless. He does not even attempt to try and alter their misguided perceptions. If you've tried for 16 years with no luck, you tend to give up. Entering a competition meant for young ladies means nothing to Pacey – except the chance to embarrass his dad.

Joshua Jackson as Pacey Witter

But like all boys, there are times when pleasing dad is all he wants to do. On the father and son fishing trip, we see Pacey set himself up to be knocked down by his father's careless and cruel words. Pacey has been scarred by the years of abuse. Reduced to a heap by the burden of his father – both literally and metaphorically – Pacey finds it's only when dad's unconscious that he can talk to him.

Even before The Change, Pacey was the best friend a boy like Dawson could have. Attentive, smart, and fun to be around, Pacey's the one who tells Dawson to get over himself when the poor guy is in danger of ruminating himself to death. Pacey's the friend who also forgives Dawson when he makes the seemingly unforgivable mistake of assuming he knows everything about his best friend. Pacey's the friend who tells Dawson to stop using words like "discombobulate" and advises him about women. He's sometimes wrong of course, but then a good friend is allowed to be wrong.

But most of the time he's right. His carefree attitude to life contrasts with Dawson's often anal attitude and he allows Dawson to shed an emotional load every now and again. Though X-ray vision was not required to see Joey had the hots for Dawson, no one was prepared to tell him, least of all Joey. So even after, in the grip of alcohol, she kissed him passionately, Dawson is still dodging the facts. It's left to Pacey with a charismatic grin and roll of his head to tell his buddy Dawson that his female buddy Joey wants to be more than his buddy. When Pacey teases Joey about her interest in Dawson, she resorts to expletives but gives herself away in the roll of her eyes. Dawson's head is so far in the clouds; he cannot even hear Pacey shouting the truth up at him. If Pacey had pressured Dawson and Joey to get together, they might have resented him post-break-up.

Pacey to Andie:
"You have no idea what you've done for me, Andie. Just being in my life. I don't know. You've made me feel like maybe there's hope for my pathetic existence."

But it's not all male bonding between Dawson and Pacey. The test of a true friendship is that they should be able to fall out, vent steam, spew volcanic lava, and still be best mates. And these two can do it. When Pacey has been – unknown to Dawson – crushed by one of his father's weighty put-downs, he gets mighty snappish with Dawson. "Screw you, Dawson. We can't all be the fair-haired walking embodiment of perfection. Not everybody has the words 'wunderkind' and 'genius' attached to our futures. Some of us are just simple-minded folk trying to get through the day without breaking something."

You see, despite his wit and quip skill, Pacey is a bit of a loner, one of those high school people who does not conform enough to fit into any of the in-crowds. This is why he gets on so well with Dawson, Joey, and later Jen as they each find the high school cliques either unbearable or impenetrable.

Although he's close enough to Dawson to ask if he looked OK on the video where he was captured with Tamara, it's interesting that he told Dawson nothing about the affair until absolutely necessary. Perhaps he did not think

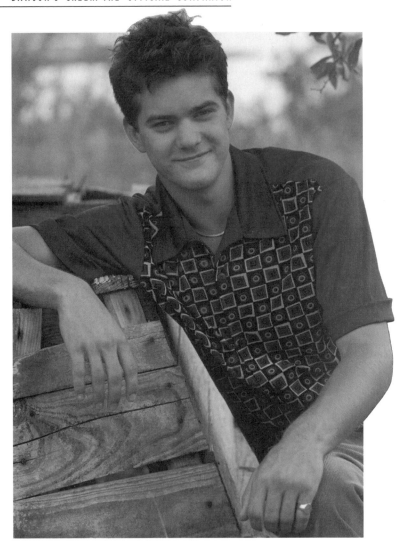

Dawson was mature enough to handle the incident (though Dawson later proves himself to be a great help) or maybe – more realistically – guys don't talk about such things unless under duress.

The affair with Tamara is far from sordid. It involved sex but it was also about a lot more for Pacey. He handled himself admirably in the face of the school board, and by exonerating Tamara proved himself to be more mature than his 15 years. Even Tamara was shocked. When Pacey's brother tries to apologize on Pacey's behalf, calling him a waste of space, Tamara has none of it and stuns Doug by saying how sensitive, intelligent, and kind Pacey is. Doug does not know what to think, especially as that is a task in itself for him. Ironically, it's Pacey who has to remind Tamara just how much he has matured when she returns to Capeside to sell her warehouse.

To Jen and Joey, Pacey often seems to be just Dawson's pal. But there are times when he's able to offer invaluable advice – not only about Dawson – but life in general.

Pacey shares a tie with Jen in that they're not as innocent as Joey and Dawson. It's not only that they're not virgins, it's also that they're a little more cynical, a little less naïve. They're both aware of the fact that Dawson is a tad too mature for his own good, both aware of the fact that if Joey and Dawson do hook up, a friendship after a break-up is a task as easy as rocket science.

To Jack, Pacey is a hero – no doubt about it. Peterson's partisan grading method is diabolical but his crushing of fragile Jack's ego was beyond words. While all the other students in the class were unprepared to put themselves on the line for someone else, Pacey was not. He's used to standing out from the crowd after all, that's nothing new. But to put his head on the block for something other than a good laugh reveals a new Pacey. Pacey's unwavering determination eventually causes Mr. Peterson to take early retirement rather than face the school board. It would be Pacey's moment of triumph – except this was merely part and parcel of The Change.

And the major Change we have been lucky enough to see in Pacey? Well, that's the way in which he managed to turn his life around. He would not have been the alcoholic pushing a cart that Andie McPhee thinks all people who miss homework assignments become, but he most certainly would not be heading toward the promising future we can now expect from him.

When Pacey learns that Dawson and Joey are at last an item, he dyes his hair in an effort to show that he too can buck the habits of a lifetime and come up trumps every now and again. And perhaps, along the way, if the gods are smiling, he may be able to win the heart of senior cheerleader Christy Livingstone. Nothing like setting your sights high. But this reinvention is as long lasting and as deep as the dye in his hair.

It is Andie McPhee – a high-strung bundle of nerves with more on her shoulders than any teen should have to bear – who helps Pacey tap strengths even he never knew he possessed. Well, what do you know, not only does his brain work, but it works damned well! And there's a good heart with lots of love to give to boot. Does this version come with any software? Pacey is a bargain and a babe as well. Though the duo start as verbal sparring partners, it was obvious that below Pacey's and Andie's smart put-downs there was a mutual attraction. Andy provides the positivity and encouragement Pacey so desperately needed, while he returns the favor by being the dependable stable in her life. One of Pacey's most touching moments comes when he confesses confusion over Andie's love for him. "Why do you like me? I'm not worth liking, Andie. I'm screwed up, I'm thoughtless, I'm insecure. Why would you want to care about me? I don't understand." Andie cares about him, as his family should, as he's worth caring about, worth investing hopes in as he gives a good return. Who else could have persuaded Andie, on the verge of a breakdown, to extricate herself from the fearsome apparition of her deceased brother?

Though Pacey is torn by her departure, everyone has confidence in him. Dawson never said a truer word than when he reminds Pacey, broken after yet another put-down courtesy of his vicious father, that there are those who realize he is more than just the joker of Capeside; this is a truly special person. And finally, Mr. Witter recognizes that which glows in his son is special and acknowledges it. Pacey has waited for this for 16 years and the moment is wordless.

JENNIFER LINDLEY
Played by Michelle Williams

Jennifer Lindley, a young lady from New York, arrives in Capeside and turns heads the moment she steps out of her cab. She has already met Dawson of course, she used to spend summers with Grams as a kid, but hey, hasn't she grown? And in all the right places too. Joey, Dawson, and Pacey each appraise the newcomer for different reasons, in different ways and they each arrive at different conclusions. To Dawson, she did not arrive in a cab, she fell from heaven. Pacey is fairly smitten as well and though he reckoned himself to be in with a chance at first, he quickly realizes that she only has eyes for Dawson. For Joey, used to male company and with no female friends apart from her sister Bessie, this newcomer is an instant threat, hustling in on her territory, flicking her blonde hair and flaunting her summer dresses like she had everything going for her.

And hey, what do you know, Jen does have everything going for her. She's full of energy, pretty, smart, sassy and possesses that which Joey dearly needs a dose of: self-confidence. Jen only tucks her hair behind her ears when the wind musses it up, not to distract attention from herself.

From the outset though, there's something unobtainable about Jen. She's seems natural, casual and carefree but she also manages to send out vibes that she's being very careful about how she's perceived. Of course, anyone moving into a new town at the sensitive age of 15 is going to be careful not to tread on any toes. She's a smart girl and does not want to stand out from the crowd. Unfortunately, it's the ones considered different – for whatever reason – who are laughed at by the lockers (Jack McPhee will tell you that in a split second). Capeside offers Jen the ideal opportunity to reinvent herself and though she at first grabs the chance with both hands, she seems to lose enthusiasm for the task as time progresses.

Jen to Abby:
"I've tried changing my image but I give up. If all these righteous teenagers are never going to accept me, then I might as well stop living this pristine and tedious existence, you know?"

Jen engages in some witty and harmless flirting with Dawson the first time she meets him but takes it only so far. Jen, after all, does not go all the way. Without even trying, she has Dawson fall in her lap, in a manner of speaking. Dawson's such a dear he not only wears his heart on his sleeve but then runs around town wearing nothing else. Yet regardless of Dawson's sincerity, for some reason, Jen holds back.

Jen's first date with Dawson cannot even really be considered a date as Pacey and Joey come along for the ride. A frustrated Joey asks Jen if she's a virgin and after a nanosecond's hesitation, Jen admits that she is. Jen begins to think that perhaps there is something more going on between Dawson and Joey than friendship but discounts that theory quick sharp as Dawson only has eyes for her. Despite these assurances, she still holds back.

Even when Dawson follows her to school dances he would not normally give up a rented movie for – she holds back. She wants to be sure. Even when Dawson challenges the Completely Perfect Cliff Elliot, Jen is overcome with embarrassment rather than enamored and makes her exit. And therein lies one

Michelle Williams as
Jen Lindley

of the key contradictions to Jen. No matter how much she tries not to be in the limelight, guys often end up making her the epicenter of their fantasies. Guys swarm to Jen like bees around honey. And though Jen should be delighted by the attention, it seems to pain her as well.

Who could forget the silhouette of a troubled girl standing by the wharf after leaving the school dance? She's gazing across the water, and even though New York's in the other direction, we're wondering what she left there that occupies her mind so. And then that guy Dawson comes and gives her a line. Except, it's not a line, is it? It comes straight from his sleeve. He does not want to be the platonic friend who hears about her boy adventures, he wants to be one of those adventures. And despite all her hesitation, all her holding back, Jen falls for him. Hook. Line. And sinker.

Joey, of course, would love to see Jen fall for someone else. Or even off something. But the thing is, she cannot hate Jen for her own inaction. Her plan may well have been 15 years in the making, but Jen naturally charmed the sleeve off Dawson. There is not a mean bone in Jen's body. She'd relish being buddies with Joey, but Joey makes her feelings clear on that point with assorted eye rolls and biting comments. When Jen attempts girl chat with Joey and reveals she's not as self-confident as people believe – she thinks she looks like a duck – poor Joey's so uncomfortable, Jen's assertion that they will be friends falls on deaf ears.

Jen only manages to get a modicum of friendship with Joey after Jen's split with Dawson. His embrace proves a little suffocating and with the fella out of the way, Jen and Joey can share a tub of cookie dough flavored ice cream. Irony is Jen and Dawson had made it through the rough times. They should have been

coasting along like a couple in a convertible along a seaside road. They had survived Jen's revelation that she was not, in fact, a virgin. They had survived Dawson pondering why Jen would not sleep with him. Their relationship was strong enough to survive Billy's divide and conquer escapade from New York. But the culmination of all these individual headaches lead to one major migraine. It was too much at just 15 years old.

The simplistic psychobabble explanation for Jen's angst would be that she wants to be loved. But she needs to feel comfortable within herself before she can be comfortable and happy with a man – this is a lesson Joey could teach her later on. Though Jen once comes close to hitting the nail on the head, the truth eludes her. "I'm sixteen, pretty, lucky, and fortunate, and way too unhappy most of the time," she says to Dawson when splitting up with him before adding that she needs to be on her own for a little while. Everyone thought she meant a few months, not a few hours. She proceeds to date guys cast in the same image – of a swamp creature. Cliff would be nice if he had a personality. Chris Wolfe is concerned with no one but himself. The rogue fisherman Vincent proves to be positively dangerous and sparks an explosion of fury from Grams the likes of which Jen has not seen before.

It is while Jen is in this self-destructive phase – drinking and partying, her looks and schooling suffering – that Dawson brings her out of her funk by making her producer of his new movie. At one drunken party, he literally saves her from herself. He doesn't accomplish this by being a boyfriend – though he tries it on a couple of times, come on, he is a teen after all – no, he saves her by being what he does best; being a damned good friend. It's her friend Dawson who provides her with a place to sleep when she's too inebriated to find her way home. Even while she's fighting the truth, verbally scratching his eyes out, Dawson works to make her see the true reasons she's turning into a heavy duty lush. It's her pal Dawson who stands beside her like the good angel while she pukes by the white picket fence.

At precisely the time Jen is turning herself around with the help of Dawson, Ty walks in. He looks as if he stepped from a clothing catalog but he proves to be not only religious but jazzy as well. Jen is smitten. And he's a good influence, calming her down and making her see that you can have a good time and still remember what you did the night before. But Ty has problems of his own that he needs to work through. He cannot deal with Jen's sexual confidence and breaks off the relationship, citing her "history" as a reason they cannot be together. Jen is devastated and reverts back to her bad behavior. As she tells Abby, she feels rejected by everyone. Unfortunately, Abby's death does not help matters. Jen's less-than-insightful eulogy so upsets Grams, she throws Jen out. Thrown out of two homes in the space of 18 months? This is not a good track record. But like the ebb and flow of the creek, Jen is one of those characters who always make a comeback. She just leaves us unsure how she's going to reinvent herself this time. And the way she does it is not to reinvent herself. Instead, she forces Grams (and, by association, all other adults) to accept she is more mature than most girls her age. Once they understand this, they can understand the true, buoyant nature of Jen Lindley.

ANDIE McPHEE
Played by Meredith Monroe

Andie McPhee is an atypical teen. She's organized and studious, takes a healthy interest in extra-curricular activities and looks both ways before crossing the road. Her Mary Jane shoes are always shiny and her hemlines are short-cute as opposed to short-naughty. She is eager, energetic, bubbly, far-thinking, and fastidious. And she cares not that her junior high nickname was Andie McGeek.

Whenever Dawson, Joey, Pacey, or Jen need advice on a school issue (with Andie, it's more likely she gives the advice whether they require it or not) Andie's the perfect person to talk to. She wants to run for student council and succeeds in making a reluctant Joey agree to be her running mate. When working on an economics assignment, Andie wants to do field research to the tune of viewing 12 apartments. Her project partner Pacey would be content to view none. She would have none of it. Andie, normally more logical than a Vulcan, makes the completely illogical leap from skipping a project to failing in life. "You get behind one day – and then you're always struggling to catch up – you get more and more confused and then eventually, you end up on the street, drunk and dirty, wheeling a grocery cart."

While the prospect of yet another school dance to celebrate yet another homecoming is as exciting as watching pastel paint dry for the rest of the gang, for Andie it's the chance to make high school memories, a chance to dress up and live the high school dream, if only for an evening. Like Jen, moving to Capeside has offered Andie the chance to re-create herself, to create the image of the happy-go-lucky student with the only thing to bother her being her grade point average.

But appearances can be deceptive. From the moment Andie crashes into Officer Pacey, we can see there's something a little bit wrong. She's sweet and penitent but there's something unnerving in the way she talks too much, too quickly. By the time Pacey's birthday party comes around, they have already settled into a comfortable battle of quick wits and sharp put-downs. But Andie also reveals how the high school dream, the parties, the laughter, the fun, and the memories seem to be contained in a bubble she cannot enter. She can dance to "Footloose" all she wants in Dawson's bedroom but a real school dance or even Pacey's impromptu birthday party proves to be problematic. Surrounded by jovial people her own age, she has rarely been so alone. It slowly becomes clear that Andie is struggling under some intolerable burden and the bright smiles, the bouncing walk, the quick wit are all her way of trying to create the façade of a carefree teen.

On her very first date with Pacey, Andie specifically tells him not to go to her house – which of course, he does. It's when Andie realizes Pacey is at her house that the last straw bears down on her already bent back. She cracks. She's so ashamed that someone has seen through her mask that she fails to

Andie to Jack:

"It's a really beautiful poem, Jack. And I don't know if it means you're gay or not. And I really don't care. But I'll tell you what I do know. The person that wrote this poem – he's as scared as I am. You're terrified and I'm your sister and I had no idea. And I just want you to know that I'm here for you. I love you, Jack. And you are not alone."

Meredith Monroe as Andie McPhee

A troubled Andie is comforted by Pacey

understand that Pacey is one of the good guys, one of those who will not judge her but support her as she comes to terms with and deals with her problems.

Grief-stricken, Andie tearfully explains to Pacey how her mother Betsy crashed the family car, killing her elder brother Tim. Her mom Betsy's grief manifested itself as a nervous breakdown and her father, unable to deal with the pressure, left soon after, providing financial but not emotional support. Her brother Jack withdrew into himself. And this left only Andie to care for the family home, her mom, and her own teenage problems.

It has to be said she has done excellently. But once her family history is in the public domain, courtesy of Abby Morgan, Andie slows down long enough to realize she's on the verge of breaking point. And that's the key to Andie. She copes and copes and never steps back long enough to recognize the fact that she may need to stop coping for a while. She only tells Pacey about her family history when her back is against the wall. She only goes back on her medication when Jack forces her to confront the fact that her mood swings are chaotic. Andie cannot do it all alone, but needs other people to point this out to her.

Thankfully, Andie knows her flaw. When Jack confesses that he is gay, admits that he has been going through a turbulent quest to find himself along with coming to terms with his family's dysfunction, she realizes the error in her tunnel vision. She has been so tuned into coping with school, coping with her mother, coping with her own grief, that she failed to see the symptoms of despair in her brother. "Everything that has happened in our lives has made me so afraid, Jack. Fear has become my sole motivating factor. And I thought nobody could understand that. Especially you, you're so independent and strong."

Andie's blossoming relationship with Pacey provides her with the kind of support she so desperately needs but it's not enough. She needs professional help as well, one with longer-lasting results than a prescription.

It is ironic that the most studious person in *Dawson's Creek*, the straight-down-the-line player – with her Mary Jane shoes and short-cute hemlines – is the only person to have a therapist! Andie's friends, the psychology-savvy crew who could tell Oprah, Ricki, and Jerry a thing or two about emotional problems and their repercussions, are not enough for her. There's not enough psychobabble in their armory to help her. It's obvious from a room over-crowded with trophies and the obsequious manner in which she seeks her father's approval that the fear of failure is so intense it means she cannot allow herself to relax for a moment. And relaxation is precisely what her therapist prescribes.

Andie took her advice, but perhaps a little too literally, getting drunk in a bar and singing the blues on stage. But she let loose. For one night at least, she was not afraid of losing control.

Andie's refusal to face the truth until it is staring her point blank in the face, or worse still, when it's too late is proved time and again. When Pacey reveals the depth of his concern for Andie, who is hyperventilating over impending finals, she says: "Pacey, I know what it's like to care deeply for someone who has the propensity to become mentally unhinged. I don't want to be that person to you. I know I'm high maintenance and I know I can be needy and anxious and high-strung, but don't take it all on yourself. Even if I ask you to – don't. It's not fair to either of us." Andie suffers a breakdown and it is Pacey, her immovable rock who is there to literally carry her. These two may appear to be star-crossed lovers – when Andie has to return to Providence, it's not only Pacey's heart that goes "boom, boom" but we know they'll be together once more. Well, we hope so anyway.

Jack McPhee
Played by Kerr Smith

Jack could not be any more different from his sister Andie if he tried. He is the ying to her yang. Upon entry to the Capeside clique Jack proceeds to make as little an impression on everyone as he possibly can. He's meek, he's mild, and he's amazingly moody. As a youngster when teacher used to tell the kids "Read quietly while I pop next door" only to have the class erupt into

chatter the moment she left, little Jack McPhee would be reading as if his life depended on it. Would that Jack had hair as long as Joey's – he would also tuck it behind his ears whenever he attracted any unwelcome attention. Though he's smart, he's so withdrawn that he comes across as moody, brooding, inward-looking, and vulnerable. His clumsiness and mediocre school performance (anything's mediocre compared to Andie's trailblazing GPA) leads people to the wrong assumption that he's no good at anything.

Jack to Joey:

"I still would have stopped [kissing Abby]. Because I realized that the minute I started that I was gay. That I am gay. It's still hard for me to hear those words come out of my mouth."

And that's an incorrect assumption to make as Jack is very good, exceedingly good in fact at listening. If there was a Listening class, preferably not taught by Mr. Peterson, Jack would be at the top. While he is trying his hardest to be invisible, to not be noticed by his family, by his friends, by anyone in high school, he is carefully listening to anyone and everyone about everything. And as we all know, if there's one thing that Capeside people love to do, it's talk.

Jack listens as Andie tries to juggle 73 balls in the air at the same time. Under the weight of her painful home life, her relationship with Pacey and her fear of failure, she begins to buckle. Jack lets Andie know when she is taking too much on, when she should perhaps consider going back on her medication. The way in which Jack learns and retains information until it's necessary to impart it is commendable. It's only when Pacey hunts Jack down to ask what's wrong with Andie (after he has dismissed her as a spoiled little trust fund brat) that

Opposite: Kerr Smith as Jack McPhee

Right: these waiters have more in common than matching outfits

Jack reveals the McPhee clan are not as well off as people imagine.

It is this skill in keeping information quiet that helps him make in-roads with Joey. He pays close attention to – and perhaps even takes notes on – Joey and Dawson arguing over the "how dare you read my journal" incident. This way, when a steaming Joey is banging around the Ice House as if she wants to make ice chips, he can offer her some pleasant advice and – shock – gain an appreciative smile. His attentive nature is further revealed in his appreciation for Joey's art. It helps that he knows what he's talking about, that he has knowledge of the artists that Joey admires. But he also takes a keen interest in Joey's art, which is different to the stuff hanging on walls. It means so much to her, more than the hobby Dawson makes the dire mistake of dismissing it as.

Perceptive as a bloodhound Jack asks Joey why she is so angry. Stunned – she resembles the con woken up by the snuffling dog – and more than a little miffed, Joey quickly replies the full moon puts her teeth on edge. "Not just tonight," he accurately adds. "All the time." When he later kisses her, he reminds us all that it's those unplanned kisses that really get you going. And definitely got her going. She reciprocated – if only for a few seconds – before remembering she was Dawson's girl. But the damage was done.

When Dawson finds out, for once he behaves like an emotional teen and slugs Jack, who does nothing, knowing perhaps that Dawson has lost Joey already. Jack is important for Joey, reminding her she's worth loving, even by those who do not know her as well as others do. Joey appreciates this and is prepared to give herself entirely to Jack. They approach the point of no return but Jack finds himself unable to reciprocate.

Jack writes the infamous poem after getting advice from Dawson on how to write something from the core of his being. The poem's ambiguity leads to a tremendous amount of stress into which Pacey dives in. It's funny then, that despite his listening skill, Jack was not able to heed the real message behind Pacey's behavior in Mr. Peterson's class. Pacey did not get himself expelled for the fun of it, he wasn't playing the hero, he actually just wanted to protect his friend. And Jack resented this, claiming he could handle his own business. Jack could not acknowledge Pacey's help as he had yet to openly acknowledge his own sexuality.

When the absent dad, Joseph McPhee, sweeps into town demanding to know the truth about his son, he ignites a powder keg. Jack has listened for such a long time, has been denied the opportunity to speak his mind for so long, that when he finally demands the right to be heard, his message hits home clearly. "Think about how you treated me and the way you treated Tim," he tells his father. "Because he was the real son, and I was different. And as hard as you've tried to stamp it out or to ignore it, I've tried harder. I've tried harder than you, to be quiet, and to forget, and to not bother my family with my problem. But I can't anymore, because it hurts. I'm sorry, Dad. Andie, I'm sorry. I don't want to be going through this. But I am."

And despite Abby trying to turn Jack back to the other side, he begins to cope with his sexuality. He even faces up to his father's prejudice and realizes he can cope, with or without parental approval. His character arc soars proudly and with the support of Jen and Grams – his new family – it will continue to do so.

Opposite: Monica Keena as Abby Morgan

ABBY MORGAN
Played by Monica Keena

To dismiss Abby Morgan as a mean-spirited girl with no redeeming qualities is more than a little harsh. There is no disputing the point that she is mean. In fact, Abby is a duplicitous, defiantly mean, miserable, catty, and conniving gossip but there's a chance there's some good in her, deep down if anyone dares or cares to try and find it. You've got to give Abby one thing, and that's her wit. This girl is quick with a quip and parents, teachers, pupils, and anything else are liable to get backlashed with her razor-sharp tongue.

Surely there is some motive to her being mean to everyone? Abby herself reckons she performs a vital function in the lives she crosses. "I serve a very crucial role in this circle and you guys are just too unimaginative to see it. I'm the girl that everyone loves to hate." But why cast herself in this role when it seems to distress her? She is good at pretending that she loves being the one everyone loves to hate but we know otherwise. Every now and again, her carefully applied foundation cracks a little and we see the real Abby underneath. The lonely Abby. Though like everyone else in Capeside, she's not afraid of talking, Abby's speech is dedicated solely to putting people down, blasting them and critiquing them. She has a way with words, this one. A cruel way. But for all her communicative skill, she finds herself unable to communicate about the things closest to her heart. It is all brash bravado and witty put-downs with Abby Morgan, when we know this stems from her own insecurity.

Consciously, she makes every effort to humiliate and belittle everyone around her but subconsciously there is something different occurring. She is begging – not just for some friends – but some friends she can trust not to betray and badmouth her the way she does everyone else. Imagine if Abby were to share an intimate secret with someone only to have that "friend" broadcast it around Capeside. Abby, more than anyone else, would feel the pain as she's done the same barbarous trick to others countless times. Her vehement dismissal of the others is really the form her jealousy of them and their honest, true relationships takes.

Though Abby strives to differentiate herself from the group she is forced to share the library with on their fabled Saturday detention, it becomes obvious she is as much a misfit as Dawson, Joey, Pacey, and Jen. You think not? Check the facts. They're all loners in their quirky little way, except Dawson, Joey, Pacey, and Jen have found something in common and have formed solid relationships with each other, which of course means they are no longer alone. They have each other to unequivocally depend on, give advice to, party with, study with, and of course, smooch. Abby has no one. She has no best friend, no buddies, no friendly acquaintants even. She tries to put wedges in between the others – she reveals to an astonished Jen that Joey is in love with Dawson – in the hopes of gaining a friend in the process. She does not even have someone to fall out with as you have to be *in* with someone before you can fall out with them! Abby needs a big dose of sympathy and not the vitriol she engenders. And because she cannot get in with them, she despises them, looks down on them, when what she really wants is to become one of them. In sister-girl's mind, if you can't beat 'em, berate 'em.

If only Abby's schoolwork received the same devotion that Dawson, Joey, Pacey, and Jen receive, she would not be collecting F's like they were in vogue. Abby works hard to put herself in the center of the unfortunate triangle which exists between Dawson, Joey, and Jen. When she has befriended Jen – something she did with no ulterior motive – and Jen confesses to still loving Dawson, Abby's disregard for Joey's feelings are astounding. Abby's incredulity about Jen's remaining desire for Dawson is expressed – as always – crudely: "He doesn't know what love is. He's a 15-year-old guy. All he knows is that he goes to bed every night jerking his gherkin and wakes up every morning, humping his mattress."

With not a nanosecond's thought for Joey, Abby advises Jen to play the slut to seduce Dawson. Unfortunately, Jen listens to her. Had she listened to herself, she would have known Dawson does not fall for such trickery. He might be fairly unaware on occasion but he is not slow on the uptake when an ex-girlfriend is wobbling around his bedroom.

Even though Jen and Abby stay friends after this incident (why do people never remember the *bad* advice friends give them?) it's obvious it will not last. The moment they have a slight disagreement, Abby will add ten pounds of dynamite to blow the incident up. They both spy the fisherman Vincent at the same time and even though Jen is not interested in him, he is interested in her. Abby's play for Vincent is blatant and childish. Jen reminds her he is probably twice her age and unaware. Abby quips: "Perfect. That means he's almost mature

Abby to Andie:
"Well, being sweet is boring. I don't have family lives like you guys. My mom's not a lunatic – my father's not in prison. I'm not the prodigal daughter from New York. My parents have an average divorce. My house is average. There's no drama, no intrigue. So you know what? I create my own drama. And I think that's a valid extra-curricular activity."

enough to handle me. I'm so sick of boys. I need a real man – with chest hair and body odor and illegitimate children scattered across the country." Her humiliation almost crackles in the air as he turns her down. Girlfriend does not cope well with rejection. She at first berates Vincent and then Jen, losing the only friend she has.

And even though they're not talking, Abby is so desperate to know what's going on, she climbs into Dawson's room to spy on Jen's first date with Vincent. Had she and Jen been friends, they would have been on the phone afterward to discuss what happens. But we already know Abby's phone rarely rings.

And ironically, Abby has some fairly astute observations to make. When she overhears Dawson's parents' arguing, she tells him: "Don't stress. Let them fight for a while, then they'll wise up, get a divorce, and everything will be better." Of course, idealistic Dawson wants his folks to stay together, but Abby is right in saying a divorce is preferable to constant bickering. But much is revealed in what Abby does *not* say. She does *not* say that at one stage she too went through the emotional turmoil Dawson's experiencing. It's easy to imagine the little Abby, perhaps even optimistic but by no means as bitchy as she is now, with a pillow over her head trying to drown out her parents' rows. Her allowance may have quadrupled post divorce but we get the impression she would rather the quarter allowance and the double parent quota. Her play for Dawson is crude and bound for failure – but that doesn't stop her. And this is all in an effort to upset Jen. It's sick.

But not as sick as her behavior during the school council elections. She digs and digs, along with the help of Chris Wolfe, who really should know better, until she discovers the McPhee family secrets. With a wonderful lack of concern, she exposes the McPhees in front of a crowded auditorium. Ouch.

And then there's Abby's investigative skills. In an effort to discover who had been intimate, she proceeds to embarrass, humiliate, and hurt everyone. It is Abby at her most skilful – devious, bargaining, psychologically keen – but it is also Abby at her worst. She's not expressed a wish to become a lawyer but it's her natural calling.

But Abby's at her most interesting when her guard is down, when she is fatigued and cannot hold up her façade of the Capeside Queen of Gossip any longer. Abby's flight down the path of self-destruction pauses when Andie realizes she sat outside the Leerys all night waiting for someone to pick her up. Despite Abby's innumerable faults, our hearts go out to her. Even Andie's cracked heart goes out to Abby. A more bitter person's reaction would have been to walk – literally – over her. Jen dismissed Abby as being incredibly mean for someone so young but at least her youth gives her ample time to redeem herself. Does she take the risk and open her heart to someone? Resign from the role of the girl who everyone loves to hate? Does she heck!

The closest thing Abby experienced came courtesy of Jen. And even Jen made her true feelings known. "I don't like you, Abby. You're a sociopath. You're malicious and you're selfish, but at the end of the day, when I look back at this god-forsaken year, the best times I've had – I've had with you." But Abby's good times are over. Permanently. Especially those she has at the expense of others, which when you think about it, are all of them. Abby's death is suitably horrific for those who believe in karma – what goes around, comes

Opposite: John Wesley Shipp as Mitch Leery

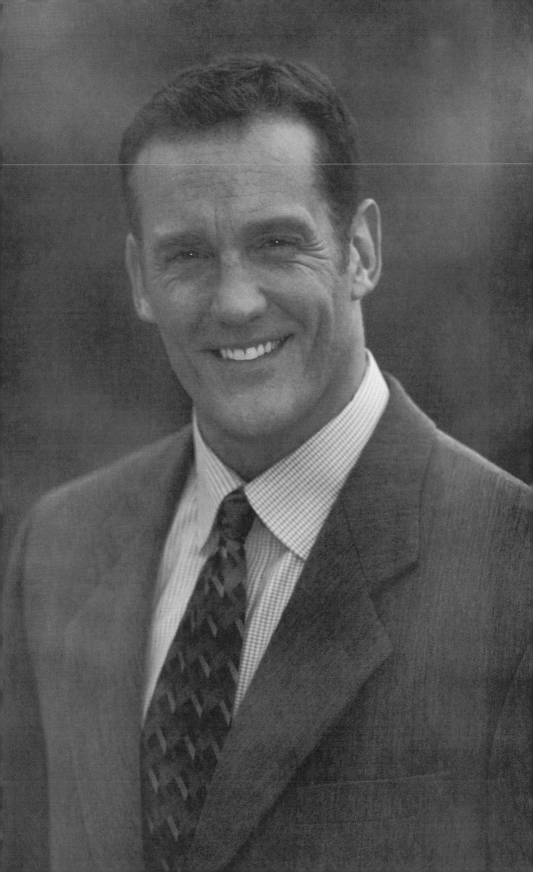

around. Abby's wide eyes reveal the terror and the dark, cold, swirling water is enough to send a chill up a seal's spine. Abby's dead! But don't forget her too quickly – we can trust Abby to haunt Capeside, scaring the eyebrows off fragile Andie.

MITCHELL LEERY
Played by John Wesley Shipp

It's when life seems it's most idyllic that it tends to throw an extra-large wrench into the works. And this is precisely what has happened to Mitch. The trouble is, he never seemed able to recover, to grab the wrench with both hands and yank it free from the cogs.

It's obvious from the way Mitch carries his shoulders that he's often plagued by moments of self-doubt. He has not worked in aeons and feels he has let his family down. But he needs to remember that the most important job he has ever held – being a father – he has excelled at. Dawson is proud of his father, looks up to him and is able to tell Mitch he loves him. How many 15-year-olds can do that?

Mitch to Dawson:
"Dawson, you can psychologically deconstruct me all you want, but here's the deal. Parent – me. Child – you."

Mitch is also able to discuss being sexually responsible, reminisce about his own days as a libidinous 15-year-old and knock down Dawson's ladder with a broad smile on his face. If all parents were as open, surely the teenage pregnancy rates would be much lower? Though Dawson feels as if he could curl up and turn crispy in the heat of embarrassment, we know he feels an eternal gratitude for having such a deep relationship with his father.

But Mitch is far from perfect. He is so thrown by Gale's affair he finds himself unable to forgive her, regardless of how much he tries. He has been betrayed and uses every opportunity to remind her of this. He is dismissive of their counselor and welcomes Dawson's attempts to psychobabble him like a condemned man welcomes an executioner. It's ironic that those who are the most scornful of emotional help are often those with the most to gain from it. But Mitch's generation is one which still holds beliefs like Men Don't Cry and Don't Show Too Much Emotion to heart. Unfortunately.

So what does Mitch do? Well, he works out, he putters around the house and he talks to friends who give him awful advice about "open marriages" and does not seem to do much else. We get the feeling that Mitch would be a lot more useful if he found something constructive to do. His restaurant dream seems to be just that, a dream. Countless meetings with realtors have led to nothing and when he gets annoyed with Gale – "I've been planning on opening a restaurant. You know that," Gale has every right to get annoyed with him right back: "I hope you're also planning on getting a loan because I'm tired of indulging the dreams of a man who can't even look me in the eye."

Opposite: Mary-Margaret Humes as Gale Leery

It was astounding that considering he's normally such a great communicator, Mitch found it impossible to articulate the depth of his pain to Gale. He instead opts to communicate with a divorce lawyer. Mitch has been through incredible highs and lows in a very short space of time. He went from living in a house the sun seemed to set opposite every night with his loving wife and son to living in a bachelor pad (they're never what they're made out to be) and having his son decline his offers to hang out together. He's lost a lot but must be commended for at least sticking in there. Dawson will continue to be proud of him.

GALE LEERY
Played by Mary-Margaret Humes

As Gale discovers "perfection obtained is a discomforting state." But once that same perfection becomes unobtainable, Gale Leery realizes how much she should have valued it. But then again, everyone has a master's degree in retrospect.

Her affair is a misdirected aim to break free of a life she thought had become humdrum. Gale presumably lies awake at night every now and again wondering what on earth she originally saw in her co-anchor Bob. He doesn't look so cute now, with his square jaw. But what has doubtless consumed Gale most of the time since her affair became known is regret. She could not say she was sorry enough for Mitch. She could not kick herself enough for breaking Dawson's tender heart. She could not cry enough tears wishing she could take those stolen moments back in favor of the perfection.

Gale to Dawson: "Since your break-up with Joey, you haven't said one word about it. Dawson, you haven't even...wallowed."

This constant regret is the reason Gale grins and bears it for a long time. She remains – in spite of all signs to the contrary – hopeful that her marriage will still work, that Mitch will forgive her and that they can begin to rebuild that which they had before. And for a time, it was working; they almost had it all as Whitney Houston sings.

What is admirable about Gale though is she shows human nature at its most resilient. She could have fallen into a depression once Mitch had decided enough was enough, which would have meant she could not work or carry out her most important duty – raise her son Dawson – but she did not. She knuckled down and got on with it. This is especially important considering Mitch does not work. When he finally gets a job teaching English in Capeside High, he has already left the house and is not earning anywhere near as much. Gale has, by her own fault, cast herself as a lone parent. She and Joey's sister Bessie have a lot more in common than either of them probably realizes.

We wish Gale would stop beating up on herself so much. She made a mistake and the fallout was incredibly radioactive but she's still a cool mom. After she has recorded a report into the buying habit of teenage girls with Abby, Jen, Joey, and Andie, she takes Joey aside and confides how she looks upon her as a daughter. To Joey, whose own mother died not too long ago, this is extremely worthwhile and bolsters her low self-esteem.

Dawson reeled after learning his mother had cheated on the father she appeared to dote on. That's a lesson no 15-year-old should be forced to learn.

He must have wondered how he could ever trust someone if it transpires that his own mother was capable of such deception. But along with learning that his mother is culpable, Dawson learns a valuable lesson: she's human and prone to make mistakes like everyone else. Dawson seems to have forgiven his mother for her mistake. Now it is up to Gale to forgive herself.

BESSIE POTTER
Played by Nina Repeta

Like a faithful geyser that erupts periodically, Bessie is prone to explosions every now and again. She is a fiery, passionate woman who always seems to have a job to do and always seems anxious to get on with the task without any procrastinating. The tire needs changing? Get down and dirty and do it, there's fish to be collected and a restaurant to open.

Bessie to Joey:

"Joey, would you please just do me this one favor and stop by the Ice House on your way to school?... And when you're there – would you wipe down all the counters – just real quick? So it looks clean. Oh, and Joey. The freezer. Could you mop behind the freezer? I can't even remember the last time we did that. Thanks, Joey, you're the greatest."

Ironically, though they may both roll their eyes at the mention of it, Bessie and Joey are more alike than they actually think. Although Bessie is confident and loud where Joey tends to be meeker, they are equally determined souls. Joey's aim to escape Capeside is so powerful, she does not want anything to get in the way of working and saving money for college, studying, and Dawson. Bessie, meanwhile, is keenly aware of her own responsibilities. She has her baby boy Alexander, Joey, the Ice House, and the family home to take of and even though she's loath to admit it, she does need help. Her mother died and her daddy's in jail and it's only she and Joey.

And though Bessie is admittedly guilty of overlooking Joey's growing pains, she makes up for it by giving her honest, workable advice whenever she can. Joey's a bit thin on the ground when it comes to female pals and when she has finally, at long last, kissed Dawson who else can she turn to but Bessie? It's Bessie who is able to tell her to revel in the joy of the occasion and even explain that the second kiss is the one she should be wary about as that's the one which has been thought about carefully.

But the sisters also have their problems. As insensitive as Bessie unwittingly is toward Joey's needs, Joey is, on occasion, as insensitive to Bessie. But Bessie gives the illusion of being as tough as old leather and able to withstand anything that life, with a better arm than the best baseball pitcher, deems fit to throw at her. An economics assignment offered Joey the ideal opportunity to praise Bessie for the admirable way that she manages to juggle home, the restaurant, and her baby boy. Unfortunately, Joey chooses a super-successful (in monetary terms) single mother, Laura Westin. And Bessie is hurt. At first, she conceals her pain, but lets it loose in a geyser gush later on. Joey is stunned she has been so insensitive, and they each apologize.

The singularly most touching moment for the sisters, and proof of Bessie's unconquerable spirit, comes when she unexpectedly goes into labor.

Spreadeagled in Dawson's house, she accepts Grams's offer of help, even though Grams disapproves of Bessie's unmarried status and her black boyfriend in equal parts. Moved at how Bessie's cries of pain remind her of her mother's, Joey has to leave the house. Dawson reminds her that Bessie needs her, needs the support of the closest person to her, and Joey challenges her demons and wins. The sisters may not say it often, but they do love each other and neither could do without the other.

Grams and Jen tackle bereavement

EVELYN "GRAMS" RYAN
Played by Mary Beth Peil

Raising a teen at the end of the millennium is not easy. Grams knows this now. She has discovered that young people today are so much more aware than when she was a youngster or even when she was raising her own children. But as time proves again and again, though today's youths are smarter, they're still likely to make mistakes. The same mistakes which were made in her youth, but definitely not with the same frequency. Thankfully for Jen, having someone behind them like Grams proves to be a godsend.

By virtue of her example and her wise words, Grams is able to teach those who are prepared to listen some valuable life lessons. Gale turns to her for advice on her crumbling marriage. Grams single-handedly delivers Bessie's baby.

And of course, Grams has many a lesson for Jen, though the young girl borrows that eye-rolling habit from Joey whenever a lecture looms on the horizon. Grams is a devout woman, and though Jen is not a believer, there are times when she finds the meditative effects of prayer useful.

Grams tries to keep Jen off the indecorous road but has to face her failure sometimes. When she catches Jen writhing on the kitchen table with her dangerous date, Vincent the fisherman, her anger crackles the air, shocking Jen on to the straight-and-narrow once again. At least, for a couple of weeks anyway.

Grams's patience is tried by Jen's eulogy at Abby's funeral though. That child is enough to make a granny skip with rage. And Grams skips all the way back to her house to pack Jen's things and put her out. When Jen pleads for understanding, Grams cries – the hurt evident in her eyes: "You want understanding? Then how about a little understanding in return? How about a little compassion for me? Not just for my beliefs, but for me – your grandmother, who would give you anything, who would die for you…" Perhaps it is what Jen needed, she certainly seems to calm down once she has moved in with Dawson and his mother.

> ## Grams to Jen:
>
> "In my day, women didn't have many options. You got married. You raised a family. But now… What a wonderful time to be a woman. You can do or be anything you want… [looking at Ty] and without a man by your side."

Delightfully though, Grams also has a few surprise lessons up her ruffled sleeves. When Ty is ranting about homosexuals, intelligently insisting that "quackers" like Jack choose to "quack," Jen becomes stuck for words. It's incredibly difficult to argue rationally with people who have resorted to animal noises. Ty, assuming that because Grams is as religious as he is, she will automatically support him, is surprised and quietened when she calmly reminds him it is not his place to judge.

The best example Mrs. Ryan sets though, is on the death of her husband Joseph. Though this is a show about youngsters and their budding lives, Grams adds a great perspective. She and her husband were married more than twice as long as Dawson, Joey, Pacey, and Jen have been in existence! Though Joseph was unfortunately completely inanimate throughout the show, Grams shows by quiet devotion that love in the twilight years of life can be equally as rewarding as it was in the beginning. Thankfully, Jen reveals her caring nature when Grams breaks down after her husband's death. She feels she is alone, but Jen dutifully reminds her she is not.

Making Waves: The Actors

Tongue twisting, sex talking, angst having, and problem solving, the **Dawson's Creek** crew are the only group of teens on TV at the moment who most teens will admit can speak for them. Even though the language the show uses has been criticized as either hyper-realistic, too articulate, a little too mature, Dawson and Co. at least dispel the myth that teens only grunt and croak their way through the oh-so-difficult years. But what about the actors? Though the cast is a disparate set brought in from around America to breathe life into Dawson, Joey, Pacey, Jen, Andie, Jack, and Abby, there are some incredible similarities between the cast and the characters. But there are also some highly interesting differences.

JAMES VAN DER BEEK
Dawson Leery

With James Van Der Beek's acting ability, the fact that Dawson talks too much for his own good sometimes is delightfully forgotten with the crispness of Van Der Beek's delivery. James has given Dawson life, created the idiosyncrasies fans love and the face of the most popular show this side of the millennium. It's no surprise that the difficult search for an actor to play Dawson culminated with James as there are uncanny similarities between the character and the actor. Even his Dutch surname means "by the brook."

Born and raised in Cheshire, Connecticut, James, 22, has noted that he grew up in a small town, just like the character he plays. The eldest of three children, James's family has always been extremely supportive of his career path.

Like the highly charged character he plays, James possesses a talent and determination that revealed itself when he was young as he had inherited his father's aptitude for sports. His father, Jim, pitched for the Los Angeles Dodgers (he now works for a cellular phone company) and his mother, Melinda, was once a Broadway dancer (she now owns a gymnastics studio). James excelled at American football and was well on his way to a successful school career. Ironically, it was a mild concussion at the age of 13 that ended his American football plans but started the acting ball rolling.

His first role was the lead, Danny Zuko, in a local children's theater

James once played Danny Zuko in Grease – with the help of some black hair dye!

production of *Grease*. John Travolta made the movie role familiar with his dark locks and smoldering eyes. We already know James has the smoldering eyes and with a little help from a bottle of black hair dye, he soon had the dark locks.

At the age of 16, his supportive mother accompanied him on the tiring six-hour round trips to New York while he auditioned for commercials. Though commercials – cereal, candy, anything – were not forthcoming, James won a role in an off-Broadway play called *Finding the Sun* written and directed by Pulitzer Prize-winning playwright Edward Albee. Although James had to balance the long journeys and the grueling rehearsals and performances, he still managed to sustain his excellent grades at school. He cites this play and the attendant trials as a mind-broadening experience.

Opposite: Katie's modeling background serves her well

After this noted debut, James went on to tread the boards in *Shenandoah* and another off-Broadway play, *My Marriage to Ernest Borgnine*. The 1995 movie *Angus* in which he played an arrogant jock, was his first silver-screen appearance. James managed to land TV roles. He has featured in *Clarissa Explains It All* (another teen with a ladder for her friend to climb into her room), and also the bubbly soap opera *As the World Turns*. From here, James moved on to a movie called *I Love You... I Love You Not*, with Claire Danes, and an independent movie called *Harvest*.

James, an excellent student, won an academic scholarship to Drew University in New Jersey to study English and Sociology. He put his education on hold though as he missed acting and it's at this time Van Der Beek won the much sought-after role on *Dawson's Creek*.

The producers were finding it an impossible task to locate the ideal person for Dawson Leery, the sensitive and smart teen, and had worn a weary route to auditions on both coasts. Van Der Beek's audition tape captured the attention of Paul Stupin and he knew they had found Dawson – barely two weeks before production was due to start.

In between filming seasons one and two James drew on his school football days to play the lead in the tremendously successful film *Varsity Blues*. The movie revolved around his character, Mox, the reluctant hero of the high school football team.

"Dawson reminds me of myself when I was fifteen," Van Der Beek has said. "He's a bit of an innocent and is frequently off in his own little world, all of which I can definitely relate to." James has also referred to Dawson – lovingly of course – as the "dork in all of us." Being an English student, James realizes that though the show's dialogue may not be entirely representative of the way teens realistically speak, the scripts do represent how they're feeling. James has said "I think kids are a lot smarter than the media gives them credit for. I think they really are a lot more aware than adults often give them credit for."

KATIE HOLMES
Joey Potter

Born and raised in Toledo, Ohio, the youngest of five children, Katie never thought she would be able to make it as an actress, in spite of her fervor. Her life in the Midwest could not be further from the hubbub of Hollywood. Her father is a lawyer and her mother is a homemaker and Katie has said: "Hollywood and its numerous success stories seemed extremely far away, from a world that I would never come into contact with."

Katie started acting in high school plays and it was while attending a modeling convention that she came to the attention of her future managers. They brought her to Los Angeles for the six-week pilot season. This is a time when the networks are holding auditions for future television shows. Katie secured the part of Libbets Casey in a movie called *The Ice Storm*. Directed by Ang Lee (who also directed *Sense and Sensibility*), the movie snatched a screenplay award at the Cannes Film Festival. Katie was not phased starring opposite renowned actors like Sigourney Weaver, Elijah Wood, and Kevin Kline and put in a great performance.

The following year, Katie remained in Toledo to play the lead in her high school's production of *Damn Yankees*. Her agents sent her tape to various studios and once the *Dawson's Creek* creators had seen it, they knew Joey was in their grasp. But they needed to see Katie read once again – this time in person.

Unfortunately, the studio unwittingly set the callback date the day her hometown play was scheduled to start. Rather than leave her friends high and dry, Katie opted to do the play and luckily, the studio was able to reschedule her callback and of course, she won the role. Katie breathes life into Joey.

Like the other cast members, Katie had to move to Wilmington while the series was in production. At just 19, she had not lived away from home before although she was set to go to Columbia University (she deferred) before she won the role of Dawson's other half.

Katie also stars in *Teaching Mrs. Tingle,* which is both written and directed by *Dawson's Creek* creator, Kevin Williamson. It chronicles a high school group who plan to kill their insufferable teacher, played by award-winning actress Helen Mirren. Holmes also starred in *GO!*, from director Doug Liman (*Swingers*) with Sara Polley, Scott Wolf, and Jay Mohr, as well as *Disturbing Behavior* with James Marsden and Nick Stahl. Currently, Holmes is in production on the *Wonder Boys* with Michael Douglas, Frances McDormand, Tobey Maguire, and Robert Downey Jr.

Opposite: Joshua received three marriage proposals when his Mighty Ducks *trilogy was released*

JOSHUA JACKSON
Pacey Witter

Born in Vancouver, Canada, Joshua decided on an acting career at age nine. His first job was an advertising campaign for "Beautiful British Columbia."

Joshua's first feature film role was in Michael Bortman's *Crooked Hearts* in 1991, which was followed by *Andre the Seal, Tombstone, Digger,* and *Magic in the Water.* He also starred in the *Mighty Ducks* trilogy as Charlie, the coach's prodigy hockey player and the team's voice of reason. Ironically, Pacey refers to this role in *Detention #106*. He has also starred alongside Jared Leto and Rebecca Gayheart in Columbia Pictures' *Urban Legend*, Phoenix Pictures' Bryan Singer-directed *Apt Pupil*, starring Ian McKellen, and in a cameo role in *Scream 2*, as a cynical film class student. It was while on location for *Dawson's Creek* in Wilmington, North Carolina, that executive producer Kevin Williamson approached Joshua with a request to appear in the film, claiming it would be a huge favor.

Joshua's other feature projects include Columbia Pictures' *Cruel Intentions*, a contemporary adaptation of *Dangerous Liaisons* set in an affluent New York prep school starring Sarah Michelle Gellar and Ryan Phillippe. He also stars in Warner Bros.' *Gossip* alongside Katie Hudson and James Marsden.

Joshua's previous television credits include starring roles in two Showtime Contemporary Classics – as John Prince Jr. in *Robin of Locksley* and as Ronnie in an updated version of *Romeo and Juliet* entitled *Ronnie and Julie*.

It was in Los Angeles that Joshua read for the role of Pacey. Not many know that he was called back the next day and asked to read for Dawson. The producers decided that Pacey was the part for Joshua, which is ironic as Joshua has said that he and Pacey are "exactly the same." He adds, "Like Pacey, I also have an offbeat sense of humor and I enjoy laughing, having a good time, and often get myself in trouble for it. But neither of us is mischievous for mischief's sake."

Josh is acknowledged as the wittiest person on *Dawson's Creek* and he brings his natural charm to the role of Pacey, the joke-cracking fast-talker with the speedy line in self-deprecation.

MICHELLE WILLIAMS
Jennifer Lindley

Ironically, while Jen is having trouble making the transition from a huge city to a small town, Michelle Williams had to do precisely the opposite. Born in Kalispell, Montana, a town which is even smaller than fictional Capeside, Michelle grew up with her commodities broker dad, Larry, homemaker mom, Carla, and her four younger brothers and sisters.

At the age of nine, Michelle's family moved to San Diego and she draws on her experiences of being the outcast at school for her role as Capeside's not-always-welcome newcomer. Michelle's high school experiences were so bad she had to be privately tutored at home. Students who refused to accept the newcomer once beat her up and Michelle says the show's hallways scenes still give her "sweaty palms."

Soon after arriving in San Diego, Michelle joined a local theater group and started acting, even winning roles further afield at this young age. Like James Van Der Beek's family, Michelle's family were supportive and dad would make a four-hour journey to take Michelle to Los Angeles auditions. At 13, she won her first role as the young alien in the sci-fi movie *Species*. She went on to make *Lassie*, *Timemaster*, and *A Thousand Acres* starring Jennifer Jason Leigh, Michelle Pfeiffer, and Jessica Lange.

Michelle mixes equal parts of vulnerability and maturity to create Jen's character. She's a knowledgeable teen but still liable to make mistakes if left to her own devices. Michelle has said in interviews: "I think a part of Jen is really looking to regain her innocence and lead the quintessential teenage life, and she wants to fit in with these other carefree kids."

Michelle, now 18, graduated from high school two years early at 16 and with parental approval, moved to Los Angeles to further her career. It was a difficult time but made the task of moving to Wilmington when she won the part of Jen much easier.

In between filming the first two seasons of *Dawson's Creek*, Michelle made *Halloween: H20*, the seventh *Halloween* film. Another Kevin Williamson project, it celebrates the twentieth anniversary of the slash-horror movie, and stars Jamie Lee Curtis.

Michelle also starred with Kirsten Dunst and Dan Hedaya in the movie *Dick*, a political comedy directed by Andrew Fleming from Columbia Pictures.

MEREDITH MONROE
Andie McPhee

As a second-season newcomer to *Dawson's Creek*, Meredith has established herself as one of Hollywood's newest rising stars portraying Andie McPhee, a troubled teen under insufferable pressure.

Born in Texas, Meredith was raised in Illinois and moved to New York to pursue acting. She later moved to the West Coast when she was cast in the television series *Dangerous Minds*.

Just prior to joining *Dawson's Creek*, Meredith completed production on a CBS made-for-television movie *Beyond the Prairie: The True Story of Laura Ingalls Wilder*.

Meredith will also star opposite Taye Diggs and Dominique Swain in the MGM feature *Depraved Indifference*. The film is a mystery/drama about a college student (Monroe) who finds herself involved with the death of a fellow student.

Meredith has returned to *Dawson's Creek* for a second season, where there will surely be choppy waters ahead for Andie McPhee.

KERR SMITH
Jack McPhee

Dashing and daring – as in, how dare he kiss Joey! – Jack McPhee has proved to be a great addition to the show. Kerr Smith paints Jack perfectly as an often withdrawn, lonely character with an interesting story to tell.

Kerr was raised in Exton, Pennsylvania. He was a prolific sports player, and, unlike Jack, he was keen on student politics, becoming class and then school president. His first drama performance was in a high school production of *The King and I.*

After school, Kerr went on to the University of Vermont and completed an

*Abby and Jen discuss
New York guys*

undergraduate degree in Business Administration. Returning to his hometown, he started a business marketing firm with his father and it dawned on him that he "hated the selling aspect, but loved making the presentations." Following this revelation, he decided to pursue acting further. His first job was as an extra in the movie *Twelve Monkeys* with Bruce Willis, and soon after he got commercial work although he had to sell his Bronco to move to New York City. After a few months, he landed the plum role of Ryder Hughes in the super popular soap opera, *As the World Turns*. His performance won a Best New Actor Award from a daytime television magazine.

Kerr has also been featured in two independent movies, *Kiss and Tell* and *Hit and Runway*, which debuted at the L.A. International Film Festival. He's also in the process of writing a screenplay, but has yet to reveal the subject matter.

MONICA KEENA
Abby Morgan

Abby Morgan, the girl everyone loves to hate, capitalizes on a reputation she worked hard to create in the first season. Abby delights in stirring up the mud at the bottom of the Creek, and Monica Keena delights in playing Abby. She revels in the role of the cute, but vicious, Wicked Witch of the West.

Born and raised in New York, Monica attended LaGuardia High School of Performing Arts – the school made famous by *Fame* – from the age of 13. Monica soon made an impression and won roles in movies like *Burning Love* and a play called *The Father* starring Al Pacino and Julianne Moore.

Monica has a long list of movies to her name. She has appeared in *Devil's Advocate*, *While You Were Sleeping* and *Ripe*. Though it may be hard to believe watching her as the demonic Abby in *Dawson's Creek*, Monica also starred opposite Sigourney Weaver in *Snow White*.

Monica also starred with Mariel Hemmingway in the TBS cable movie *First Daughter*, as the president's daughter who is kidnapped and held hostage.

Dawson's Creek Sites: On Location

With its picturesque creek, the twists and turns of which mirror the lives of the imaginary town's inhabitants, Wilmington, North Carolina, is an ideal location for Dawson's Creek. It might give the impression of being a sleepy little town unused to the workings of the Hollywood film industry, but the town has a long history with movies and TV shows. As well as Dawson's Creek, it has also been the setting for such films as Firestarter and The Hudsucker Proxy and television shows like Matlock and American Gothic.

Considering Kevin Williamson based *Dawson's Creek* on events from his life, it's fitting the show's locale is a small town similar to the one he grew up in. Though Capeside is supposed to be in New England, it is actually a seaside town with a population of around 70,000 in Wilmington, North Carolina. Williamson also based his smash-hit movie, *I Know What You Did Last Summer* in the state. Wilmington is about a two-hours' drive from Williamson's hometown of New Bern, North Carolina.

Dawson's Creek creator Kevin Williamson grew up in similar surroundings

The Leery home: site of many an angsty discussion

Season two's opening sequence, with James, Katie, Joshua, and Michelle cavorting on a beach and at Dawson's house, was shot in mid September 1998 on location at the Leery house and on Wrightsville Beach, near Wilmington. Using two handheld cameras, it was deliberately given a "rough around the edges" look to make it appear as if an unseen friend was filming the gang at play.

It takes seven days to film one episode – and this does not include weekends. With such a hectic schedule, it makes sense for both cast and crew to live in Wilmington while the show is shooting. Everyone has apartments throughout the town though guest stars who are only appearing in one episode stay in hotels. Despite having pads in the town, the cast rarely get to stay there over the weekends as the busy bees are flying to Los Angeles or New York for interview commitments and to promote the show.

Wilmington producer Greg Prange, says: "The location's a character in itself. Although some characters, like Joey, are desperate to get out of the small town – 'I gotta get out of here!' – there are many people who tell me they'd love to live in a small town like that. Where else could you have a ladder safely against the wall. Small towns have lower crime rates."

The exterior of Capeside High School is actually the University of North Carolina. What many fans do not realize is that the interiors featured on the show are actually recreated on three enormous sound stages some miles away in the town. One stage is dedicated to the high school and Andie's bedroom, the one cluttered with the thousands of trophies. The second stage houses the Leery home, the one where the doors are always being slammed. The third sound stage features Grams's house, Dawson's bedroom and Grams's and the Leery's porches, two of the busiest porches in television. So when we see Dawson running out of his house, the interior shots will have taken place on the soundstage and the exterior shots will have been filmed at the house itself. Now that's smart.

Dawson's Creek's Creators

Dawson's Creek *is undoubtedly a smash hit, but did you know it's the first television show that wunderkind writer Kevin Williamson has made? He was yet to make his sharp-talking, attention-grabbing smash hit movies* **Scream, I Know What You Did Last Summer** *and* **Halloween: H20** *when one of his scripts came to the attention of a Columbia TriStar executive. It burst open like a ripe melon with rich dialogue and great plots. Though that script was for the movie* **Scream,** *Williamson was keen to break into television. A talented group of people were drafted in to create a reality out of a dream: producers, directors, writers, casting agents, and costume designers. Here, they each tell their own stories and how* **Dawson's Creek** *has affected them.*

KEVIN WILLIAMSON
Creator/Executive Producer

Kevin Williamson may be in the fast lane of Hollywood with hit movies like *Scream* and *I Know What You Did Last Summer* under his belt, but it's clear *Dawson's Creek* is a personal triumph. It's no secret that Dawson is Kevin in his youth, before the writer – who was himself a huge film fan – surfed the waves of success.

Kevin, now 34 years old, grew up in the small seaside town of Oriental in New Bern, North Carolina, similar to fictional Capeside. In fact, Dawson's Creek is an actual place near Oriental where Kevin would impress dates. With touching honesty, Williamson and the show's team of talented writers give an unsurpassed spin to the intriguing and poignant story of a group of teens coming of age. The basis for Dawson and Joey's taut relationship is his own friendship with a girl called Fanny Norwood though it was Kevin who had the pneumatic crush on her.

Like Dawson, Kevin thought director Steven Spielberg was a genius and he emulated him in movies he would shoot in his backyard. He also encouraged his school librarian to take out a subscription to *Variety*. He left Oriental to pursue an acting career in New York in 1987 but soon relocated to the West Coast. There, he worked as a music-video director's assistant, took a scriptwriting course and wrote screenplays on the side. He submitted scripts to studios for a few years before *Scream* won the attention it deserved. The script also piqued the interest of a Columbia TriStar executive, Paul Stupin. A meeting to discover whether Williamson had an interest in television developed into the runaway success of *Dawson's Creek*, the number one show among teen girls in the U.S.

Named as an Entertainer of the Year for *Entertainment Weekly* in 1997 and listed on *Premiere* magazine's Power 100 list for 1998, Kevin has other projects simmering away. As well as the horror flick *The Faculty* and *Killing Mrs. Tingle* (which he also directs) he is also developing a twentysomething L.A.-based drama called *The WasteLAnd*. It has been described as characters from *Dawson's Creek* placed in the fast-paced environment of L.A.

Kevin's characters possess a wit and charm rarely seen on-screen. The characters of *Dawson's Creek* and the way they tackle problems – both normal and not so normal – has enchanted millions around the world and here Kevin takes us into his world and explains how the show came to be:

Does Dawson Leery talk too much?

Does he talk too much? Well, since I talk too much, I'm just going to say "No," he's just very articulate!

Did you talk too much as a teen?

Of course not! Er… yes, every step of the way.

One gets the impression that *Dawson's Creek* is very close to your heart – is that the case?

Oh my God yes! It's close to my heart in every sense. I've become more involved emotionally as in the course of making the show, all the actors and writers – I've become great friends with. James, Katie, Josh, Michelle, Kerr, Meredith – I'm passionate about them. They're an amazing group of kids and I think of them as family. Because I work so hard I don't really have an outside life. I'm in love with these kids and I am very maternal that way, I'm their caretaker of sorts – and they take care of me.

You once said fear was the motivation to write – fear of not being able to pay your bills. Can this have been the case with *Dawson's Creek* considering you had already sold *Scream*?

The motivation behind Dawson's Creek *was that it was a chance to do something very personal, semi-autobiographical.*

The 1997 *Time* article by Michael Krantz said: "Williamson's kids may talk like therapists, but they act like guarded and wounded 15-year-olds whose cellphones and videotapes stand in for a

sadly absent adult institutional authority." Is that a correct assessment?

That's cynical but there is a layer of cynicism that rides through the show. While I do think it's an accurate interpretation of one aspect of the show, there is a lot more going on than merely a layer of cynicism. The cynicism is found in other characters. I have a great cynicism that runs through me, it's my defense mechanism. Joey is our cynical character. She has a huge heart but she was a little more wounded than Dawson; she thought he had the perfect world, that kept her a little angry and a little hostile, which gave her spunk and fire and made her Dawson's soulmate. It's interesting that Dawson is learning. He began with this idealistic perfect family but from the first episode he realized it was not so perfect and thus cynicism was born and his coming of age came to pass.

Did you always have the idea for a television show?

It was one of my first meetings after I sold Scream. That movie had been such a big to-do that I was thrust into the Hollywood fast lane. I was just this small town kid who didn't quite know, I had all these ideals of being a filmmaker and I went in to meet Paul Stupin and he was thinking about an anthology horror series. I explained I wasn't really a horror guy. He said, "What do you mean?" and I explained that I don't really do the horror thing, it was just part of my childhood. Paul asked me what other stories did I have from my childhood. I told him I used to hang out in a small little town and make home movies in my backyard and then I started weaving a story about a girl down the creek who used to row over on a boat and it was very much my life. I created a tale around it sitting in the room. He asked me to come back the next day and pitch an idea and I stayed up all night and figured it out. I created a tale about all my friends and all the characters are based on me in some way or another.

How similar are you to the Dawson we see on screen?

James Van Der Beek is certainly much better-looking. But Dawson and I are very similar in the way we analyze everything far too much. Just like Dawson I am profoundly self-aware to the point where it sometimes renders me clueless. We're both idealists and passionate about what we do, we're both in love with cinema and have an unconditional love for Spielberg. We both believe in romance, we both believe in hand-holding and sweaty palms and knees getting weak when you kiss someone you care about. We're full of a love for life and we've both made mistakes along the way.

Kids today have more knowledge of TV psychobabble than ever before – how do you think this has shaped them and how do you write for such an audience?

I don't seek out to write for a younger audience. I sit down to write the stories that I want to listen to and watch. I think that's one of the reasons that it works for a younger audience. They're complimented instead of being thrown in a group in a box and given entertainment specifically for them. I just try to write smart, savvy, entertaining characters who happen to be 15 or 16 years old. It's not my goal to write just for kids, I want to tell smart stories to a smart audience.

There's an episode (*High Risk Behavior #210*) which features much pondering on Dawson's part about his own script and whether or not it is true to life – did you ever go through these doubts?

That was a ribbing of ourselves. We were having fun with some of our criticisms, at how overarticulate the characters are. There's a fantasy element to the show. But it's also realistic in terms of the way kids talk, feel, and how we express ourselves. There's a fantasy element as we're able to go there with the dialogue and respond in a way that most of us wouldn't think about until we got home that night and we were lying in bed. We can let our characters come up with it right on the spot.

In effect, you and other crew members are living a Dawson dream as you're able to edit moments from your lives, embellish the good ones and edit the uncomfortable moments?

Oh yes! There are so many moments in Dawson's Creek that have come right out of my life. I think that's true of the other writers as well. We will sit around and chat and tell a story about what happened yesterday in the car wash or 15 years ago and then it's a storyline in Dawson's Creek.

Could you envisage the series running and running, creating a whole life for Dawson, perhaps as his film career takes off?

I'm so tired right now I cannot even envision him getting out of high school! But if we were so fortunate as to have the show run that long, Dawson would have to pursue his dreams at some point.

You could have decided to make it *Cliff's Creek* and based the show on the all-American high school hero Cliff Elliot who's perfect, intelligent, varsity quarterback, class president. Why did you then base it on Dawson who detests extra-curricular activities?

The whole point was that Dawson is the underdog in the external world. But he's everything in the internal world. While a lot of this character is me, a lot of him is who I wish I had been. I get to relive my past in a therapeutic way and make it better. The others are already into their futures. Joey's a grade "A" student. One of the great things in season two is to see Pacey turn himself around. He went from slacker to getting his first "A" which was an emotional moment. They're anti-school in attitude but they're very responsible kids.

It's no secret that the relationship between Dawson and Joey is based on your relationship with your best friend called Fanny. Have you spoken to her since the show first aired?

Fanny and I have been in touch. We got in touch when the show first aired. I hadn't spoken to her in ten years, she now lives in San Francisco. We talk regularly and try and see each other when we can, we're good friends.

With Dawson and Joey, they moved beyond friendship. With many shows' characters – like *The X-Files* or even *Superman* – it is the

unconsummated passion which keeps viewers enthralled. How has *Dawson's Creek* managed to maintain viewer interest even after Dawson and Joey hooked up?

Hopefully, that's what being a storyteller is all about, diving into the world of fiction. We have to keep that tension going and come up with new and exciting ways to create conflict – that's what the relationship is founded on.

How do you respond to the criticism the show sometimes receives about its sexual content: Jen losing her virginity at such a young age, Jack's homosexuality?

We're going to get our fair share of criticism thrown at us whether it is a sex episode or if Dawson gets a "B"! I've never had any politics or creative concerns from anyone that works with the show. I've had nothing but support in every storyline that I've told. The trick is to not worry about the storyline and whether you're being responsible to the issue you are dealing with. The important thing is to respect and honor your character and their choices and decisions. That way, you cannot help but be responsible because you're being responsible to the character and the issue.

What has been – for you – the most touching scene from the show?

In Be Careful What You Wish For *#216 at the very end Dawson explains to Joey why he got drunk. He basically said it's because he's lonely. There's a theme of loneliness that runs through the show. Jack has admitted that he's gay but now he has to accept it. And for him at first, that's a very lonely thought. Then we see Gale and Mitch struggling with their marriage and we get the impression that they are two lonely people. And then we see Jen reject a man and once again enter into the world of loneliness. That theme is just so personal and powerful. We've got people of 16 dealing with this. At 16, Dawson is profoundly lonely and he comprehends it and all he can say in his saddest moment is "I love you Joey." And for me, that's one of our most powerful moments. It goes back to the pilot of the show – which is the heart – and it's all about the window.*

And of course, Dawson's self-awareness makes his pain all the more poignant.

Exactly! He's so self-aware he recognizes and announces that he's lonely – however it's one of those moments where the feelings overcome him and it makes his place a painful place to be.

Joey rolls her eyes at Dawson's idealistic nature. Is she right in thinking he is destined to be hurt until he toughens up?

I think she's rolling her eyes because she's hiding her idealism. I think she's just as idealistic as he is and that's their connection. She would like to believe that she's rolling her eyes to tell him that until he wakes up and smells the coffee he is going to be clueless and hurt and in pain but her eye-rolling is her defense mechanism.

Opposite: Dawson holds Joey's attention

PAUL STUPIN
Executive Producer

Paul Stupin, *Dawson's Creek* executive producer, draws on a super library of knowledge he has built working on other shows.

An English graduate, Paul's TV career began in series development at NBC in 1984 as director of drama development. Paul has also worked on Hollywood movies, while vice president of production at TriStar Pictures. His credits include *Steel Magnolias*, starring Julia Roberts and Sally Field, *Short Circuit* starring Ally Sheedy, and *Nothing in Common* starring Tom Hanks.

Returning to television in 1989 with the Fox network, he then helped to create another famous teen show, the glitzy *Beverly Hills, 90210*. As well as producing *Dawson's Creek*, Paul edits the material for Dawson's Desktop, the on-line companion to the show. Here, Paul tells us how he chanced upon an interesting script:

"An executive producer's job is to develop interesting ideas and put them with fresh writers. Once the season starts, it comes down to the mechanics of making sure it gets made.

I first heard the idea for Dawson's Creek *about three and a half years ago. I was developing new shows and I happened upon a draft of a script called* Scary Movie. *I loved it, there was great suspense and the thing that struck me about it was the quality of the youthful voices, they were very witty and well constructed.*

I still remember that day in my office reading that first draft of Scream. *I called Kevin Williamson — it was his script of course — and luckily he was interested in talking about television. His career was just starting off. He came up with the idea of doing a series. In my mind that was the perfect area for him, his characters were very smart and articulate and perfect for the genre.*

Kevin went off to think about the potential series. He sketched out the concept of Dawson's Creek *— every character was so vivid that I knew right then and there that we had something really special. We took the idea to Fox, where I used to work, and we pitched it to them. They bought the idea for Kevin to write as a script and even though it was the best I had ever had, they passed on it! They did not see the potential that we did. Six months later the Warner Bros. Network took up the idea for* Dawson's Creek.

The casting was a long process. We saw Katie's video, cast her as Joey and then cast the other actors. We saw hundreds of actors and still had no lead. We saw everyone in Los Angeles, then we started searching elsewhere. We were two weeks away from shooting and still had no Dawson. Then my casting agent got hold of this video of a young actor and dispatched it to my house. The cassette got stuck in my VCR! I got another tape, looked at James Van Der Beek and knew we had our Dawson!

Because Williamson molded the series around events from his life, it personally means a lot to him. It possesses a degree of reality and emotion. It also has a lot to do with his imagination and storytelling. The show succeeds on the strength that it is fresh. These are unique characters and there was not an honest, smart series about the lives of four young people. The originality of their voices had a lot to do with it. The visual look of the show plays an important part as well. We shoot in a beautiful part of the country and try and make an effort to show the scenery.

The gang display their sense of style

The core of our series is the relationship between Dawson and Joey. For our show to be fresh, that relationship has to be interesting. Over the course of the first season we saw Joey deal with pent-up emotions all year. At the start of the second season we wanted Dawson and Joey to hook up. The relationship was rife with conflicts, after all, they were in a powerful relationship for the first time in their lives. As season two progressed the relationship did not work out. They have gone a long hard road to re-establish their friendship. The key to keeping the show appealing is to keep the relationship unpredictable. Our characters are sophisticated and intelligent. The emotions are universally identifiable and people can relate.

We gained viewer trust through three areas: first, the quality of the stories and writing, secondly, as a direct result of the actors. We have an ensemble of youthful faces that light up the screen. They're remarkably talented. They're capable of grabbing an audience's feelings. Our third strength is our direction. Each director does a wonderful job in visually translating each script, and in creating beautiful tableaux with the characters and the environment. With Dawson's Desktop, we can expand on each episode. The Internet is also a great forum for people to communicate. I sign on after each episode as it gives us a hook into what our fans like about the show and what they don't like and what they're discussing. It helps plan how we're going to proceed.

As well as executively producing the show, I also choose the music. Everyone makes suggestions and it's great that we can use contemporary music. I like it to be a mix of new music and stuff that is breaking on the radio. I want people to go mad and wonder what that song was!"

GREG PRANGE
Supervising Producer, North Carolina

It's Greg's job to keep all the elements of Dawson's Creek – the scripts, director, crew, and cast members – running smoothly while on set.

Born in Detroit, Michigan, Greg, 47, has been a producer, editor, writer, and director during his long television career. His credits include shows such as The New Adventures of Flipper, Angel Falls, and Nash Bridges.

A father of three, he has an instinctive knack for relating to young adults and he recognizes that the appeal of Dawson's Creek is that it does not belittle its viewers in any way. He says:

"It's my job to creatively allow everyone to do the best work they can do for us. I also creatively steer the show in production. Dawson's Creek is shot in the small town of Wilmington, North Carolina.

My first impression of the show was that it was something really special. I have teenage kids so I know how hard teens are to please! We don't talk down to viewers of the show and they respond to this.

Dawson's Creek tackles issues that are important to people, but at the end of the day, it's a show about people. You don't have to be a teenager to watch Dawson's Creek. You've got the dynamic of the parents' storylines but we also try

to speak to the human voice in all of us. Everyone has felt those moments of pain, loneliness, or joy. People can relate to Dawson's Creek whether they are 18, 40, or 50 years old.

Teens today are more aware than they were before and this manifests itself in a number of ways. Even ten years ago, there were perhaps 20 television stations. Now there are 150 stations on a satellite dish. As the world gets smaller, the amount of information that is available to everyone is huge – especially young people – as they are so hungry for it.

Though teens are more worldly now, they still experience the same things as teems in the past; the adolescent years of growing up and finding out who they are. Today, they're often smarter and their vocabularies are better because they have more information available to them.

It was daring of the show to tackle the fact that Jen lost her virginity at the age of 12, but I believe the generation of teens we have today are more conservative. I think it was wilder when I was a teen than it is now. There's so much comment about how much more liberal television and film are today. Twenty years ago it would be taboo to show a condom if two teenagers were having sex even though it shows they were practicing safe sex.

One of the funniest moments we've had on set was where Joshua and Katie were wading through the water. It was terribly cold as we shot that scene in November. The cold was the downside but the upside was that the alligators were hibernating! Had the water not been so cold there would have been sharp shooters and the actors would not have been in the water. When we scouted the scene we had to have our vests on as it was hunting season and we didn't want anyone to shoot us!"

ELLIE KANNER
Casting Director

Casting director Ellie Kanner has been with *Dawson's Creek* since July 1998. She has the task of matching actors to the roles and descriptions given by the show's producers. It was her job to find the actors to portray the roles of Andie and Jack McPhee, and with the help of Kathleen Letterie, head of casting for the Warner Bros. network, Ellie found the ideal young talent, Meredith Monroe and Kerr Smith respectively.

With her partner, Lorna Johnson, Ellie also casts the guest stars for *Dawson's Creek*. These are the additional actors that appear in one or more episodes but not every one. The second season's most memorable guest stars included Chris Wolfe (Jason Behr) and his precocious little sister Dina (Brighton Hertford). Andie and Jack's parents also made a rare appearance, Betsy McPhee (Caroline Kava) and her absent-without-leave husband Joseph (David Dukes).

With ten years of industry experience, Ellie, 33, is renowned on the Los Angeles entertainment circuit. She has cast the pilots of *Friends, Clueless, Sabrina, the Teenage Witch* and co-cast the pilot of *Lois & Clark: The New Adventures of Superman*, as well as various feature films.

Born in Hartford, Connecticut, she moved to Los Angeles and has worked as a talent agent since then. Ellie has also found time to co-author an indispensable book for hopeful actors called *Next: An Actor's Guide to Auditioning.* She says:

"Our producer, Paul Stupin, calls us to let us know about a character and we start thinking of actors who'd be appropriate for the role. We then put out a 'breakdown,' which is a description of the character and any additional requirements we need of the actor, (e.g., dialects, if they're needed to play the piano, etc.), to all the talent agencies in Los Angeles. The agents then send us pictures and résumés of the actors. My partner and I go through them and decide who to bring in for an audition.

We like to bring in about ten actors to audition for each role. If we're adding a new series regular, like Meredith (Andie) and Kerr (Jack), we would have several casting sessions with our producers and audition hundreds of actors ourselves. For a guest star part, due to time constraints, we will only have one or two weeks to cast the role.

Some actors will be a little different than what the producers originally asked to see as the requirements may change while the writers work on a script rewrite. If we're looking for an actor to play forty to fifty years old, we might bring eight actors this age and two a little younger, or a little older – just in case.

My partner and I auditioned over fifty girls for the role of Dina Wolfe, Chris's little sister. The girl who won the role, Brighton, came in with the right attitude, energy and confidence. When we saw her we knew she was capable of playing this part.

Producers are always busy so we'll only show them our top recommendations. In a given day we may audition anywhere from one to fifty people. The actor has usually studied but not memorized the material. He then reads the scene with my partner or myself. If we feel the actor is physically right for the role but hasn't given their best audition, we'll give them some direction and have them try it again. After the audition, the actor's agent will often call us and ask for feedback. We try to be as honest and helpful as possible. Some actors are bad auditioners but brilliant actors. Most actors are nervous no matter how many years they have been auditioning.

Sometimes we'll put a few actors on tape and send it to the producers (Paul Stupin and Kevin Williamson) and then call back those actors that they feel are appropriate. After the callbacks, the producers may request a 'demo reel' of their top choices. This is made up of various TV and film clips of the actor's work. In less than ten minutes, you can see a variety of roles that an actor's played. Usually the actor will ask the producer of a project for a copy of the episode/film to use on the actor's reel. Then the actor hires an editor to put the scenes together.

After a discussion, the producers will decide which actor they'd like to hire. We then call the agent who represents the actor and negotiate a deal. If for some reason the actor becomes unavailable, (e.g., gets another job while we were making our decision), we may have to hire our second choice.

The production office then arranges to fly the actor to Wilmington. In casting Dawson's Creek we try to find great actors that are not too recognizable, but have a lot of experience.

Even though Kevin Williamson is an accomplished actor, he's not going to be appearing in any upcoming episodes…but you never know…"

ALONZO WILSON
Costume Designer

Alonzo Wilson, 33, was born and bred in Wilmington, North Carolina, the actual town where *Dawson's Creek* is filmed. He attended high school there and knows the fashion and style of the residents better than anyone!

Always interested in theater, he relished the opportunity to work in New York and launched himself into the business as a costume designer. His job involves more than simply dressing the cast, for it falls on his shoulders to create a style for the whole show.

Alonzo's television credits include Oliver Stone's *Heaven & Earth*, *American Gothic*, *The Road Home*, *In a Child's Name*, and a period drama called *The Ditch Digger's Daughters* for which he had to design clothes from the 1920s through to the 1970s. Wilson has also worked with Academy Award-winning actor Anthony Hopkins on *The Road to Wellville* and the first *Ninja Turtles* and *Mortal Kombat* movies. Alonzo says:

"I've always kept Wilmington as my home even when I was living and working in Los Angeles. My mom and dad and most of my brothers and sisters — ten in all — still live here so it's nice to be working here.

On a show like Dawson's Creek, the producers and I sit down and have a discussion about how we want the characters to look. We live and shop in Wilmington when the show is shooting. It's a very small town, but as quaint and beautiful as it is, it's challenging to maintain the variety of characters' wardrobes. But I do try to shop in the town as much as possible.

It might seem like Joey wears those short shorts all the time, but when it gets cold she doesn't wear them! The producers had an idea of how she should look. Fortunately Katie's very cute and we're able to get away with the tank tops and the short shorts for as many scenes as possible. It's a little sex appeal and the guys would be like 'Oh, there she is!'

The producers were very nice and let me get a hold of the characters in my mind and establish their look based on things I could get here in town or on a short shopping trip. I don't need to make myself crazy trying to get clothes from both coasts. We don't go for the real expensive clothes — they should be accessible to teenagers. Here in Wilmington, I've been able to accomplish this and still keep it real and accessible to teenagers who may not have a lot of money but like one of the tops, for instance, that Joey wears. Every once in a while I go out of town for Jen's character, since she has experienced New York and I wanted to bring a little of that flair here. Andie came from a "country club" past so I keep her preppy with cute little Mary Jane shoes. The actors have done catalog shoots and I was glad to know the style we had created was the same image the catalog had. It reconfirmed all of our hard work.

We had to shoot one scene where the characters had to jump into a swimming pool fully clothed. Meredith was brave enough to jump in wearing a skirt, but we didn't think to weight the skirt. She was real embarrassed as the skirt floated up and there was her bum! The director left it as it was — he didn't reshoot the scene — and the editors worked around it, so you don't actually see anything."

Bringing in the Net

Dawson's Creek on the Internet

Most Dawson's Creek viewers suffer from terrible bouts of periodic information withdrawal. With the close of any episode, there comes the knowledge that a whole week, seven days, 168 hours has to pass before the next instalment. We need to know everything about the atypical, angst-ridden teens in New England. Luckily, the show's creators came up with the ideal way for people online to obtain and devour more information about Dawson and his garrulous associates.

A simple, well-constructed fansite would not be enough for most *Dawson's Creek* viewers; they would want the same high level of production online as on-screen. Luckily, Columbia TriStar Interactive has established an interface more powerful than anything seen on the web.

DAWSON'S DESKTOP

By logging on to **www.dawsonscreek.com**, fans are able to view the contents of Dawson's computer – his e-mails, his scripts, his chat rooms, his favorite sites, and even his trash bin. Intermittently, we become privy to information he may not have yet revealed, or has no intention of revealing, to his best friends or family. There are tantalizing new stories and plots online and Dawson's Desktop allows surfers the chance to point, click, and discover what makes Dawson tick.

The Internet has become both a barometer of a show's appeal and an ideal way to expand its network time slot. The key figures behind Dawson's Desktop explain how the project is put together.

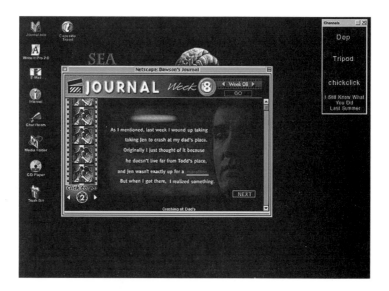

Dawson's Desktop
transforms your
computer into
Dawson's workstation

ANDREW SCHNEIDER

Director of Marketing for Columbia TriStar Interactive

Andrew Schneider, 27, has a master's degree in interactive telecommunications from New York University. Columbia TriStar Interactive was created in 1994 to explore ways of making television and other media interactive. The Sony Corporation (the parent company to Columbia TriStar Television) has a reputation for blending entertainment and technology and this department is an extension of this belief. Andrew previously worked for NBC and was responsible for establishing that network's online presence early on. He has been at Sony Pictures Entertainment for two and a half years and recognized the potential for *Dawson's Creek* after creating its website based at Columbia TriStar's homepage. He says:

"I've always had a passion for telecommunications and this way I can combine my two favorite hobbies, television and computers! I saw the potential

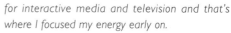
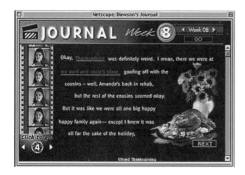

for interactive media and television and that's where I focused my energy early on.

Richard Glosser, the president of Columbia TriStar Interactive, recognized the need to get into the online arena, and we started creating promotional websites for film and television. We saw that Dawson's Creek *was a phenomenal hit and we came up with the concept of this Desktop and pitched it to the studio and the show's producers.*

Dawson's Creek *fans are very loyal and seek out information about the show and the stars. Internet fans are perhaps our best fans and we want to support them. We recognize their talent and their enthusiasm. We took a look at the Internet and* saw literally hundreds and hundreds of Dawson fansites. The majority of these sites had something called 'fan fiction' where they wrote their own episodes for fun. We wanted to offer them something they could not get anywhere else. We wanted to offer more of the Dawson's Creek experience to online users, so not only could they get more of the story, they could participate in the characters' lives. Our other challenge was to channel the online users back to the show each week. This called for very tight integration between on-air and online. All week, when the show is not on-air, we tease visitors with plotlines so they watch the show and they're more invested in the Dawson's Creek experience as a whole.

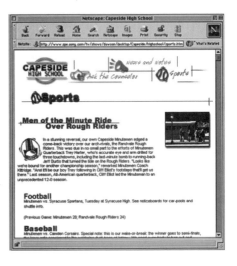

Last summer we logged around 300 Dawson's Creek fansites and noted which ones we liked. Now, there are over 500 sites. When we developed Dawson's Desktop, we invited twenty-five creators of the best fansites to be our Advisory Board members. We're in touch with them all the time. We wanted to make sure the fans were getting what they wanted. They helped us design the interface and they told us what they liked and did not like. We also wanted to make sure that we kept everything real.

The competition from these other sites does not pose any problems at all! We're very flattered and embrace our fans. They've taken the time to build some wonderful sites in honor of the show. We monitor the web to the best of our ability. If there are any extreme infringements we would ask the webmaster to stop. We release materials that the studio has sanctioned for the building of websites and it has a license agreement attached to it.

The site was up and running by September 1998. A part of Dawson's Desktop is Virtual Capeside. We built Capeside.net as if it was an actual website and you can go and explore the town, the businesses, and the school. We're encouraging people to come in and build their own virtual residences. So, if you wanted to build your own virtual home next to Dawson's we would provide assets for you to download and build.

Every week we send out an e-mail newsletter, called Dawson's Scoop, to our subscribers – we have over 100,000 at the moment. It highlights what's going to be on the show each week and also what's on Dawson's Desktop. It also features interviews with producers of the show, who provide exclusive behind-the-scenes information.

Every week we pick a fansite and feature it in the newsletter. We have a ton of banners and graphics for fans to post on their sites so they can say they're part of the official Dawson's Creek web ring.

We chose this format for the site, as we wanted to build a website that did not look like a website. We wanted to build something where everything was taken literally. We wanted to immerse you in the Dawson's Creek experience and tell the story from Dawson's perspective. His desktop is a window into his world. Another reason we chose the Desktop is that we wanted to also use the Internet as part of the environment. We're able to use every kind of software and website that's out there – through the use of hyperlinks. That opens up a whole new technology for us to use, as well as marketing opportunities and product placements.

We're creating a new model site that in itself is based on fiction. This means like film and television, we can use product placement. We do have traditional ad-banner rotations as well. But the desktop environment opens up opportunities for sponsors to place their products.

We get a tremendous amount of e-mail from people who do not receive the show in their country but who are able to follow along, via the website – which is great.

The Town Hall area of Dawson's e-mail allows the online community to come in and participate. The Internet is not a one-way medium as opposed to television and every other medium out there, apart from stand-up comedy! People can interact with us, they send us e-mail and we respond to some of it. We encourage people to role-play and though people can talk about the show, the stuff that Dawson replies to is that which is done in the voice of the show.

We're on Capeside time, not real time, so we don't shut down! The story lines will continue and we archive all of our content so if someone wants to go back and find the online episode that corresponds to the on-air episode, they can.

It was a challenge to execute our vision and make it a seamless experience. We're using dynamic HTML and rich media but minimize the heavy download times. We also have a custom-built time delivery system for his e-mails and we use a great deal of Java Script. If you're on the desktop for five minutes it seems as if Dawson is there with you. The chat might open and he will start chatting with a friend or he'll open his word document and start writing. The spirit of the site is to cross over – hopefully a character from Dawson's Desktop could appear on the show."

Catch up on Capeside news

ARIKA MITTMAN
Dawson's Desktop Writer

For those who have not visited the site, Dawson's Desktop is a completely interactive website which transforms your computer into Dawson Leery's, allowing you to get close to the expressive teenager. Created by Columbia TriStar Interactive, it allows you to trawl through Dawson's journal, e-mail and wastebasket, flip through his scripts-in-progress and, if you're lucky, even eavesdrop on some of his live chats.

Arika Mittman, 24, writes all the text on the website as well as being a writer's assistant in the executive producer's office. She is responsible for creating the e-mails Dawson receives from his friends and school colleagues, and even friends and relatives we have never seen on the show!

Born and raised in Long Island, New York, Arika went to college in Connecticut. There, she wrote for theater and gained valuable experience fulfiling internships in television before graduating. She then moved to Los Angeles, and worked in casting before pursuing her first love: writing.

She assisted in the first season of *Dawson's Creek* and while the show was in between seasons, she worked on a pilot called *Wind on Water*. Arika returned to *Dawson's Creek* for the second season and relished the opportunity to involve herself with the indispensable online companion to the show, Dawson's Desktop. She adds:

"In September 1998 the producers hired an outside writer to do the Desktop but then decided to have someone who was involved with the show – as they would know the voices of the characters better. I was excited and a little nervous at first but it's a fabulous opportunity. It's a different medium than most writers are used to. I had never done anything for online publications before. I was overwhelmed but the guys at Columbia TriStar Interactive were great and put me at ease.

You can send Dawson an e-mail

I give my material to executive producer, Paul Stupin, for approval. I write the e-mails, chat rooms, and journal based on the previous episode and the one it precedes. I try and hint at things that are about to happen. The important thing is that it's Dawson's reality, so we do not include things that Dawson does not know – it has to be from his perspective.

Although the role of Dawson's Desktop was originally publicity for the show, it has taken on a life of its own. It's not just a sideshow, it does not just recap what has happened. At first, I wondered if people would even be able to get onto it and now we have over a million users per week!

They spread out the content throughout the week so it looks as if a real week is going by for Dawson and he is receiving e-mails and working on scripts.

I worked a little at making an online persona for Dawson. You have to think about who this character is. But you have to think about what they would do online. It's a little different from what they do normally. The technical people wanted to have a homepage for Joey but I said 'She wouldn't have her own page, she probably wouldn't own a computer high tech enough!'

I had used the Internet for research and e-mail but didn't surf that much. I had never used a chat room, and so, doing research for the Desktop, I had to go into one. I found it pretty dumb! The people weren't talking about anything. The chat rooms that I write are obviously an extension of the show and so feature super intelligent chat!

Dawson's scripts-in-progress make interesting reading

The site has an appeal that's distinct from the television show and that's because the show's external. The Desktop is Dawson's internal world and we see what he thinks. This appeals to core audience viewers, as they want to feel closer to him. It's not snooping, but the thrill of getting closer to him, you're part of his inner world, sharing his most private thoughts. We get the chance to see what he says to people who aren't in the show. We get to see what he says to Nina, the girl he met in Rhode Island in the "Road Trip" episode from the first season. We even have characters that have never appeared in the show and I hope we may be able to bring one of them into the show one day.

I write the material in the same way that a writer writes a script. You hear the voices of the characters and think about what they would say to certain people, what they would be willing to admit. Some stuff is a little close to the edge but it's not that risqué. I'm not really subject to the standards and practises that the writers are – although obviously there are things that would be inappropriate.

The Town Hall section of the site enables viewers to send their own e-mails to Dawson. We get lots of e-mail that says: 'Dawson, you don't know me but I have a crush on you.' We don't always put up e-mails that are nice but we have to keep the reality of the site and won't have an e-mail that says 'I hated what happened in the last episode' – it has to sound like an e-mail that Dawson would receive in real life.

Kids today are more aware than they were in the past and that's the appeal of the show. Even if the kids aren't that smart, they want to be. The characters in the show obviously have great vocabularies, they don't really talk like teens. To some degree Dawson's Creek represents what some kids would like to be like. If they could choose, they would choose to articulate themselves that well."

THE TOWN HALL HAS MAIL

The Town Hall section of Dawson's e-mail offers surfers the chance to comment on the show, its characters, and plots. But in keeping with the role-playing nature of the site, they're also able to act as if they're Capeside residents. Perhaps they work in the salon or sit behind Dawson in his economics class. Here is a selection of real e-mails, written by visitors to the site.

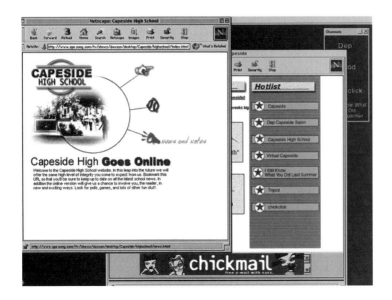

Find out who got good grades in Mr. Peterson's class

Hey Dawson,

I just wanted to say I hope you have a wonderful Christmas! I also wanted to update you on my current project. Just as you are making a movie, so am I. I was wondering from one filmmaker to another, would you be interested in teaching me the ways of your special effects and by the way… Who is your agent? I need one. I live in AZ. Talk to ya soon.

Dramafreek

Dawson,

Hi. how's your film coming? Joey told me about it. Do you know who I am? You probably don't. I'm in Joey's art class and we have Marine Bio together. It's so nice of you to give her half of the money. I mean she told me that she didn't want to take it from the budget from your new movie but she really appreciates it. Did you hear? She went out with Jack McPhee. The new guy. I think that he's kind of cute so could you maybe set us up? Cuz I know you still have a thang for Joey. Well I'll C Ya Later,

Jessie

PS If you don't get together with Joey anytime soon, give me a call.

Dawson,

Hi it's me Krystal! I go to school with you…you probably don't even know who I am… just wanted to say that I know that you and Joey broke up. I am always the last to know. I am really sorry about that. Well I wanted to let you know that I kind of have a crush on you. You are just so adorable. Well hopefully I will hear from you soon. Keep in touch!

Love Krystal

Hey Dawson,

I have no clue if you'll have the slightest idea who I am but what the heck. I lived in Capeside until I was 12. We were friends at a young age until, if I recall correctly, I told you that I thought E.T. was a stupid movie. I think you yelled something about me being a mentally impaired moviegoer and Joey kicked me. Then the two of you ran off to your house. Well I read an article about Joey and Dawson winning the Boston Film Festival. Congrats! Anyways if you recall who I am drop me a line. I'd be interested to hear from you.

From Katy

Dawson,

So I managed to get a hold of your script and read it. I must say I'm impressed. Can I give you some constructive criticism though? My one main thought was the fact that it seemed to jump a bit too much. I found myself changing my internal channel more often than I wanted to, and at times it seemed to get a bit on the perplexing side. All in all though – cheesy title and character names aside – it was a well written and thought up piece of work. Good luck with it :o)

As ever,

Christin :o)

Eavesdrop as Dawson chats to his pals

Hey Dawson

I would just like to give you some very good advice, DON'T GO THERE WITH JEN!!!! You will regret it because she is bad news. You're too good for her anyway.

Anonymous

Dawson

You need to give Joey the space that she has asked for. Just bond with Pacey and Andie or something… Let her have her fling with Jack and soon I'm sure she'll realize you are the one for her…

Love, Elaine

59 Dawson,

I know things look bleak now, but don't give up. I have it on very good authority that you and Joey will be back together very soon :) I also want to comment on the sad state of affairs that has led to your parents' separation. Don't despair, behind every gray cloud is a silver lining. You have the power, strength, and conviction to survive anything that befalls you. Okay, now I sound like one of those cheesy Hallmark greeting cards. Oh well, enjoy the weekend Dawson.

Your Secret Admirer

The Gang at a Glance

Learn the who, what, where, why, when and how of the major characters at-a-glance. Here, you can quickly gather the modus operandi of the major players in the show and even the things they're least and most likely to say as they go about their incredible, inexhaustible interpersonal relationships.

DAWSON LEERY

Nickname	Call him **Oompa Loompa** at your peril
Parents	**Mitch** (mostly unemployed, spent most of his time working out at the gym, finally got a teaching job at Capeside High – how embarrassing) **Gale**, news anchor, had affair with co-anchor, Bob, cue divorce
Siblings	None, which is why Dawson behaves like a spoiled kid sometimes
Boyfriend/Girlfriend	Went out with **Jen** thinking she was the one. She broke up with him, then he realized **Joey** was the one. She then dumped him for Jack, a gay guy (though she never knew he was gay at the time!)
Most embarrassing moment	Turning up drunk to his own 16th birthday party, catching the gay guy making out with a girl on his bed and making a humiliating speech before falling into his own cake. Oh yeah, his mom took back the brand new car she had bought him
Most triumphant moment	Kissing Joey for the second time. The first time he was dared to do it, the second, well, that was his own initiative. There is also the completion of his movies, a real talent this guy
Worst character trait	He thinks too much and does not go with the flow, more octogenarian than teen

Best character trait	His sensitivity. Dawson remains, despite the angst, the best friend anyone could have. His counsel proves invaluable to all the people he knows
Least likely to say	"Now that I think about it, Spielberg never did grow out of his Peter Pan hang up!"
Most likely to say	"My inertia is profoundly unattractive. No wonder Joey dumped me. The only worthwhile thing I did all last year was realize my feelings for her, and then I couldn't even hang on to her." *Be Careful What You Wish For (#216)*

JOSEPHINE POTTER

Nickname	**Joey**
Parents	Mom – died of breast cancer Dad – well, he was in prison, then came out, but will go back in again
Siblings	Sister **Bessie**, who takes care of her baby boy and manages the family restaurant, The Ice House, where Joey (and Jack) also work
Boyfriend/Girlfriend	She has had feelings for **Dawson** for some time but repressed them throughout his infatuation with Jen. But her feelings exploded at the end of season one as did Dawson's – whoah! That was a hot kiss. Also takes a boat trip with **Anderson** in *Kiss (#102)* and shares tender moments with **Jack** before he reveals he is gay
Most embarrassing moment	Realizing the boyfriend she had kissed in front of a crowded corridor was gay? Having her family history bleated to a hall full of students while running for student council? Have spoiled little rich girls dismiss her as trailer trash in a beauty competition?
Most triumphant moment	Getting Dawson after years of pent-up angst. But there is also the fact that she was brave enough to finish with him to try and "find herself." Joey's art is also very important
Worst character trait	Her lack of confidence, when, in fact, she's the smartest, cutest, nicest – you get the picture
Best character trait	Her faithful determination. Joey may be preoccupied with fear about her future, and even though she studies like crazy aiming to get out of town, she also knows the value of her friendships
Least likely to say	"I wake up every morning glad to be in this town, it's flora and fauna and inhabitants provide me with no end of joy!"
Most likely to say	"A neighbor girl dumped you, no one died. Get over it." *Road Trip (#108)*

PACEY WITTER

Nickname	None
Parents	Dad **John** is Capeside's Chief of Police. He's an amiable guy to others but belittles Pacey continually. We never hear about Pacey's mom
Siblings	Three sisters. An elder brother **Doug**. Pacey calls him Deputy Doug and teases him about being gay (though this is unconfirmed). Doug once pulled his gun on Pacey. Very worrying
Boyfriend/Girlfriend	After the affair with his mid-thirties English teacher **Tamara Jacobs**, Pacey recovered well and is now most attentive toward **Andie**
Most embarrassing moment	Many to choose from; being left out at his own 16th birthday party? Having to stand before the school board and pretend he had been lying about his affair with Tamara? Having his own father berate him for not being more like Dawson?
Most triumphant moment	Getting rid of the Evil Teacher, Mr. Peterson. Pacey collected testimony from pupils, researched teacher ethics, and swept Peterson, the principal, and the school board's legs right out from under them — you go, boy!
Worst character trait	His self-deprecating manner may be amusing but stems from a serious lack of self-confidence
Best character trait	His wit. This boy's surname suits him well and even when he's in a funk, he comes quick with the quips
Least likely to say	"Now that I think about it, Mr. Peterson did have a good teaching technique!"
Most likely to say	"Please don't make me eat dinner with the Stepford Family." *Beauty Contest (#111)*

JENNIFER LINDLEY

Nickname	**Jen**
Parents	Father and Mother are in New York
Siblings	None
Boyfriend/Girlfriend	Quite a few. Jen is considered to be the bad girl in town though it's obvious she's seeking attention with her revolving door of boyfriends (**Billy**, **Dawson**, **Cliff**, and **Ty**), drinking, and partying. She's a smart girl but unlike most characters, she seems to lack any definite ambition
Most embarrassing moment	Though we never saw the incident, getting caught fornicating on your parents' bed ranks pretty high on the humiliation scale. Or there's realizing that after breaking up with Dawson and seeing him fall Big Time for Joey, she wanted him back
Most triumphant moment	Turning herself around. With the help of Dawson, Jen cleans herself up again after she falls back into her drinking and partying ways
Worst character trait	Jen has a bit of a mean streak that she fails to conceal sometimes. Flaunting herself in an effort to win Dawson verged on cruelty to Joey. Dawson resisted though
Best character trait	She knows how to cut loose and have a good time. When she's good, she's good. When she's bad, she's bad. But when she's in a good mood, she could show party animals a thing or three
Least likely to say	"Tell me that Bible story again, Grams, the one about that Job guy. It just cracks me up!"
Most likely to say	"Please Dawson. Save me the character dissection." *The Reluctant Hero (#208)*

ANDIE McPHEE

Nickname	**Andie McGeek**
Parents	Her mother, **Betsy** is suffering a nervous breakdown Her father **Joseph**, has more or less abandoned the family
Siblings	Her brother **Jack**. Her other brother **Tim** died in a car crash; cue family crisis
Boyfriend/Girlfriend	**Pacey**. He provides a stability she craves
Most embarrassing moment	Having her family history announced to the entire school, as one example of Abby Morgan's vicious campaign tactics. Also crashed into Pacey, mistaking him for a cop and having him berate her as a "little missy" who can't drive
Most triumphant moment	Getting "Officer" Pacey back by having a luscious cheerleader agree to go out with him only by thinking he was going to pop his clogs at any moment
Worst character trait	Her uptightness. If she spoke any faster she would have to be recorded and played back at slower speeds so folks could understand her
Best character trait	Her love for school. Not only academically but the extra-curricular activities as well. She's a go get 'em gal and isn't afraid to let you know it, go go Capeside High – yahoo!
Least likely to say	"I know gang, let's drop everything, skip school, and take a drive in my Saab over to the next town and have some fun!"
Most likely to say	"Look, [Pacey] I know there are a dozen dim-wit 'C' cups with highlights you'd rather be speaking to right now, but you're the only person I know in Econ and here's the deal. I left my bookbag in my locker yesterday. So, if you don't mind, could I look at your notes on the Econ reading?" *Alternative Lifestyles* (#203)

JACK MCPHEE

Nickname	None
Parents	Um… the same as Andie's
Siblings	**Andie**, who is seen as holding the family together. Poor Jack is going through troubles of his own and has been suffering in his own bohemian and withdrawn way for some time, he's the strong silent type
Boyfriend/Girlfriend	He went out with **Joey** for a while before acknowledging he was gay
Most embarrassing moment	Being forced by evil teacher Mr. Peterson to read out loud a poem he had written with homosexual overtones. Now everybody knows his business
Most triumphant moment	Holding his head up in the school hallway while everyone pointed, laughed, smirked, and hid their secret admiration for his bravery
Worst character trait	His clumsiness; give this kid your prized nude still-life sketches to look at, and he WILL spill something over them
Best character trait	His optimism. In the face of crumbling plans, Jack always seems to have a positive outlook and is even able to give good advice to people who seem a lot more assured about things
Least likely to say	"I have a problem with nudity."
Most likely to say	"Romantic. That's kind of a nice word for 'loser' right?" *The Dance (#206)*

ABBY MORGAN

Nickname	**Satan**
Parents	Her mom and dad are divorced, but thankfully, her allowance quadrupled
Siblings	None
Boyfriend/Girlfriend	None – wonder why?
Most embarrassing moment	Being exposed as a lying, cheating, vicious little witch who, even if she did have redeeming qualities, would not allow anyone close enough to find out what they were. She was the one kissing Jack on Dawson's bed, just to see if she could "turn" Jack
Most triumphant moment	Not handing in a project on the sex lives of her classmates – perhaps there is a soul to save after all
Worst character trait	She persists in hurting those who try to be kind to her. Abby is – in psychology terms – a heavily defended mind, and does not reveal the extent to which her dysfunctional home life hurts her. Her mother once forgot to pick her up for eight hours or so, ouch!
Best character trait	Her wit. If there's one thing this girl can do, it's make you laugh till you see stars. She speaks slowly and clearly so you can hear every cutting comment and vicious verb – wonderfully bitchy, a sort of wicked witch of the West, East, North and South
Least likely to say	"I am truly, truly sorry guys for all the mean things I have ever said to you over the years – I really mean that!"
Most likely to say	"I can't believe I'm friends with someone who only has eyes for Dawson." *Alternative Lifestyles (#203)*

Also available from
Andrews McMeel Publishing:
THE DAWSON'S
CREEK JOURNAL

Available at your local bookstore
To order call 1-800-826-4216